1 *John Wark hooks the ball home in Amsterdam.*
2 *Tension on the bench as Town hold on against Alkmaar.*
3 *Triumph and delight for Mick Mills.*
4 *Next morning, a delighted Bobby Robson reflects.*

5 *Preparing the book: Phil and David look through Pat Edwards' albums.*
6 *They visit Pat Godbold and see displays of memorabilia at Portman Road.*
7 *Wendy Felgate has dozens of photos of her late supporter mum Betty on tour - here (left) outside Colditz Castle.*
8 *Andrew Houseley (right) ensures the project is a family affair.*
9 *Ian Hunneybell in Luxembourg gathering material for his travelogues.*

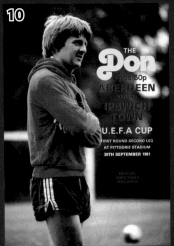

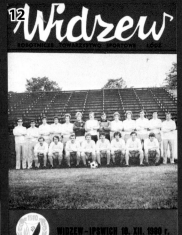

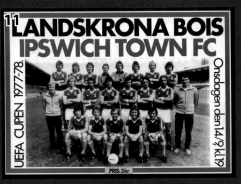

10 *Away Programmes*
- Aberdeen.
11 *Landskrona Bois.*
12 *Widzew Lódź.*
13 *Avenir Beggen.*
14 *Floriana.*

15

Кубок УЕФА 2001/2002 г.,
1/64 финала розыгрыша
(ответный матч)

«ТОРПЕДО МОСКВА»
(Россия)

«ИПСВИЧ ТАУН»
(Англия)

Олимпийский стадион
«ЛУЖНИКИ»

27 сентября 2001г.,
четверг, начало в 21.00

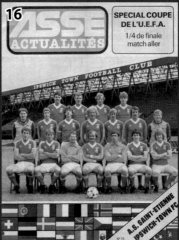

16

18 ΑΡΗΣ   ΙΠΣΟΥΙΤΣ

ΤΕΤΑΡΤΗ 1 ΟΚΤΩΜΒΡΙΟΥ 1980
ΚΑΥΤΑΝΤΖΟΓΛΕΙΟ ΣΤΑΔΙΟ
ΚΥΠΕΛΛΟ ΟΥΕΦΑ.

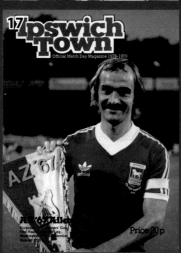

17

19

15 *Torpedo Moscow.*
16 *St. Etienne.*
17 *Alkmaar (Home - Cup Winners Cup).*
18 *Aris Salonika.*
19 *FC Barcelona.*

20 *From David and Phil's personal collection.*
21 *The Club's commemorative pennant.*
22 *A smaller version of the UEFA Cup on permanent display at Portman Road.*

1 *Inside the Luzhniki Stadium, Moscow.*
2 *Intrepid travellers (from left to right) – Phil Taylor, Martin Beecroft, Ian Hunneybell and Jon Craig.*

3 *Town fans get into character in Helsingborg.*
4 *Ian swaps caps with a Swedish fan before the game.*

6

5 T*The Town fans came to the San Siro with hope and a few toys.*
6 *Even Bluey gets in on the act.*

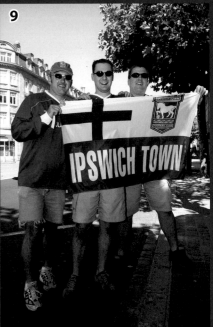

10

11

13

12

7 *A panoramic view of the Stade Josy Barthel, Luxembourg.*
8 *Holland and Wilnis up for the ball vs. Avenir Beggen.*
9 *A warm August day in Luxembourg.*
10 *FK Sartid's recently built stadium.*
11 *(Left to right) – Jon Craig, David Bull and Ian Hunneybell make it to Smederevo.*
12 *"One-nil to the Tractor Boys."*
13 *Colourful ticket for the Sartid match.*

14 *Darren Ambrose signs his autograph at Prague airport.*
15 *The thick black line in Liberec.*
16 *Preparing to defend their 1-0 lead in Liberec.*

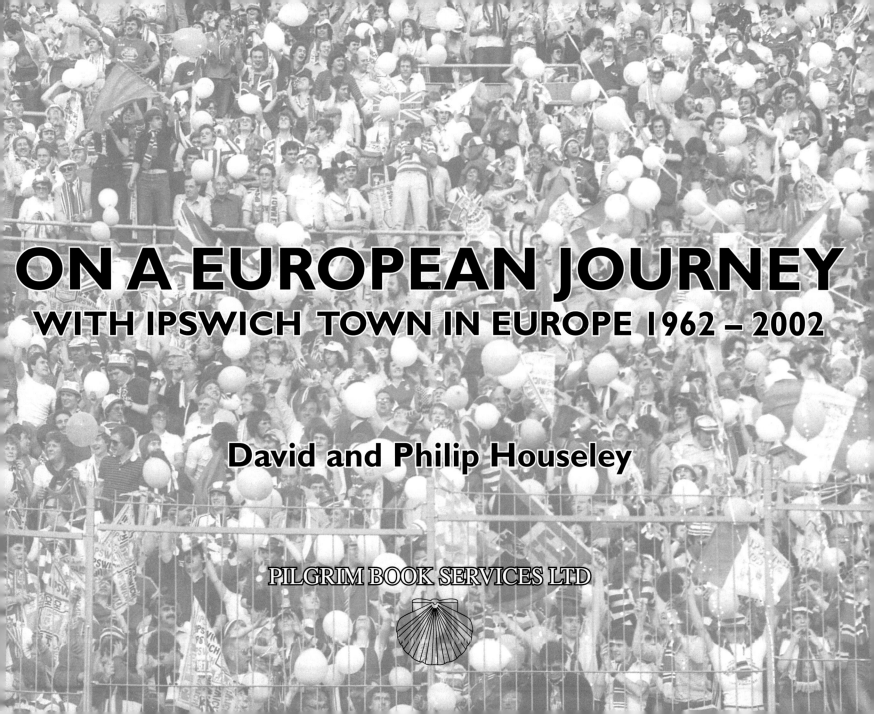

ON A EUROPEAN JOURNEY

WITH IPSWICH TOWN IN EUROPE 1962 – 2002

David and Philip Houseley

PILGRIM BOOK SERVICES LTD

ISBN 978-0-9532511-9-3

Published by Pilgrim Book Services Ltd,
PO Box 27, Woodbridge, Suffolk, England, IP13 9AU
www.pilgrimbooks.com

Cover design by Fielding Design
Typeset and production by Rupert Wheeler
Printed in China

Cover pictures (Clockwise from Top): John Wark scores his goal in the 1981 UEFA Cup Final 2nd leg; Fans show their support on the piste at Innsbruck 1978; Setting sail for Europoort and Alkmaar 1978; Cooper and Gates run with the Cup in Amsterdam; Fans at Stade Josy Barthel for the game with Avenir Beggen 2002; Bobby Robson leaves the Town Hall with the silverware.

Acknowledgements

The publishers would like to thank Archant Suffolk, Ipswich Town Football Club, The Press Association, Colorsport, Mirror Group, and David Kindred for their kind permission to produce many of the photographs. The remaining photographs are with grateful thanks to Ian Hunneybell, Graham Chenery, Pat Edwards, Jill Lewis, Wendy Felgate, Peter Slater and Alan Reed. The Cartoon by Roy Ullyett is reproduced with kind permission of *The Daily Express*, with the assistance of The British Library (Newspapers Section). Newspaper extracts are reproduced with kind permission of Archant Suffolk.

The authors and publishers wish to express their sincere thanks to the following for their assistance and imparting their knowledge during the preparation of this book: Ipswich Town Football Club, in particular Pat Godbold, Terry Baxter, and Hannah Macaulay; Archant Suffolk, including Terry Hunt, Sharon Clark, and Katie Lunnon; Bobby Ferguson for his Foreword and his recollections; Ian Hunneybell for his articles on the recent European games, and his proofreading; Gerry Harrison, Stuart Jarrold, Peter Slater, David Kindred, and Owen Hines; Richard Powell; Terry Baker and Paul Voller, among others, for their help with statistics and photo captions; Tony Scarff, Keith May, Pat Edwards, Jill Lewis, Geoff Dodson, Graham Chenery, Brian Polson, John Booth, Wendy Felgate, Tony Shaw, and all the fans who contacted us with memories and offers of help.

Every effort has been made to contact copyright holders of material which appears in this book. The publishers and authors apologise for any errors and omissions.

Introduction

by Philip Housely and David Houseley

It is difficult to realise that it is going to be thirty years – in May of 2011 – since Ipswich Town captain Mick Mills lifted the heavy UEFA Cup on that memorable night in Amsterdam's Olympic Stadium. Yet 30 years it will be, and the several thousand Ipswich supporters who were there, will agree that it was a night they will never forget.

But there were a lot of other memorable nights on the way there, over that period of ten years when Town were in Europe every year bar one – and indeed in the earlier years, a decade before that, when Ipswich supporters could sample the delights of Malta and Milan – though that was before the era of package tours and charter travel.

It was not just the matches themselves, but also the getting there - and back again , that brings back memories. There was such a spirit of camaraderie, friendship and common purpose among those travelling together on coaches, ships and planes, that the journeys were a real part of the experience. This was especially true of the occasions when we chartered whole ships for the journeys across the North Sea to Belgium and Holland.

The major factor – as members of the Press and media so many times reported – was the almost total lack of friction, violence and drunkenness among our people. This was often put down to the fact that we were the peasants from the backwoods of Suffolk – *ie* The Tractor Boys of yore – who didn't know any better, and wouldn't lift a finger to anyone. Of course, we knew perfectly well that it was simply our nature to act as reasonable human beings. But the record for good behaviour was one we became very proud of, and it was clear that this was true of virtually all of those who travelled with us – they were just as proud of the record of Ipswich Supporters as were the Club and the players, and it was the ordinary travellers and supporters who would take the first steps to stamp out any potential flashpoints before they ignited.

We thank all the many people who have responded to our request for their memories and anecdotes of their travel experiences, many of which are recorded in this book – but also to those whose stories we were not able to include – in the main because a lot of them said the same thing, "we had a wonderful time; we saw some great football; we met a lot of marvellous people who supported our opponents; we also drank a lot and we sang a lot, and we cheered our team on all the way."

Isn't that the way football should be supported?

Foreword by Bobby Ferguson

Throughout my time with Ipswich Town, I was always acutely aware of how important the supporters were to the successes the team and the club achieved. It's not just the volume of their support in the stadium, but the terrific enthusiasm they always displayed - and that was, quite simply, infectious. This level of support does get through to the players and it means that they will pull out that little extra something that can make the difference between winning and losing. In short, everyone at the Club knew how important they were and appreciated this very much.

It was particularly important to have that kind of support when we played away from home, and whether in England or in Europe we were exceptionally lucky to have so many loyal and ardent fans behind us. When we were involved in European games, it was a difficult time for British football, with so many examples of hooliganism breaking out involving British fans in a number of European locations, and I know that a number of our opponents were quite apprehensive about the trouble they might be facing when our people arrived for the game at their stadia. But our fans were to show the way that football should be played and watched - quite a few coaches and directors of opposing clubs congratulated us after the games on the way our supporters had handled themselves, and we as a Club were very proud of them.

So I am delighted that this book has been produced to record that decade, and more, of European glory from the point of view of the supporters who travelled to the away games. They were obviously very well organised, and being civilised Suffolk people, they were perhaps less likely to give trouble than some others might have – but I know that the arrangement of all those tours did involve a great deal of thought and planning.

I also know that all those who have contributed their memories and stories of their travels with Ipswich Town to this book, are still good supporters of the Club, so I wish them all the best and hope there will be more European glory to come for the Town in the not too distant future.

OPPOSITE
1962 – The Champions come home.

IN THE BEGINNING...

Season 1962-63

European Cup
Preliminary Round

September 18th 1962

Floriana Malta 1   Ipswich Town 4

September 25th 1962

Ipswich Town 10   Floriana Malta 0

In the Autumn of 1962, Ipswich Town, under the stewardship of Alf Ramsey, found themselves the Champions of England because in the previous May they had won the First Division Title for the first time. One of the consequences that no-one at the club had really thought through was that the club would be representing the country on an international basis, in that they would be competing in the European Cup.

When the draw was made for the first round, which was in fact the Preliminary Round, Ipswich found themselves up against Floriana of Malta – one of the smallest clubs in the smallest country in membership of the UEFA continental body.

The game in Malta was played on September 18th. The whole experience was new to most of the team – several of them had never flown before – and staying at the five star Phoenicia Hotel was rather grand – although they came down to earth a bit when they discovered that they would have to change at the hotel as the Floriana ground had no changing or showering facilities! Ipswich showed their superiority by winning 4-1.

The second leg was played at Portman Road only a week later, and resulted in an emphatic Town win by no less than 10 goals to nil with Ray Crawford scoring five of them and Ted Phillips scoring twice, as he had in Malta. This of course was the high-striking partnership that had terrorised the defences of the English First Division in the previous season. This aggregate score of 14-1 was a record in European competitions at the time. The Maltese were rather shell-shocked; their goalkeeper blamed playing under floodlights, and others said they were not used to playing on such a fine grass surface, nor in front of a crowd of 25,000.

LEFT
Stand-in captain Ken Malcolm exchanges pennants with Floriana's Demanuele whilst Swede and his young assistant stand guard.

First Round

November 14th 1962

AC Milan 3   Ipswich Town 0

November 28th 1962

Ipswich Town 2   AC Milan 1

In the next round, the first round proper of the competition, Ipswich were given a much tougher draw – against AC Milan, with the first leg to be played at the awe-insipiring San Siro Stadium – although the atmosphere could have been a lot better, with a crowd of only 7,600. Most Milanese had never heard of Ipswich and did not know where it was. Their team included several of the top Italian players, including Cesare Maldini, who later became one of the country's most successful managers, and Gianni Rivera. Also playing was Giovanni Trapattoni, who was appointed Replublic of Ireland manager in 2008 and former Italian team manager. Also playing for Milan was Jose Altafini, who in this season went on to set a scoring record of 14 goals for European competitions, a record that was equalled in the 1980-1981 season by one John Wark. Suffice it to say that Ipswich lost 3-0, although they managed a very creditable win by 2-1 in the home leg, helped considerably by the

support of the 25,000 crowd. AC Milan went on to win the European Cup that season, beating Benfica (Eusebio and all) in the final.

It was to be another ten years before Ipswich Town once more had a taste of European football but the supporters had enjoyed this preview – even though there was at that time no organised arrangement for supporter travel. Most importantly, Ipswich supporters now knew that all things were possible – and although they had been rocked by the sudden departure of Alf Ramsey to take on the England job – the announcement came right in the middle of their European campaign, though Ramsey did not finally leave until the end of that season - they looked at their club with fresh eyes, and greater expectations of things to come.

RIGHT
Alf Ramsey

THE ROBSON
YEARS...

Season 1973–74

UEFA CUP
First Round

19th September 1973
Ipswich Town 1   Real Madrid 0

3rd October 1973
Real Madrid 0   Ipswich Town 0

The Town, having finished the 1972–73 season as runners-up in the First Division, found themselves, under the leadership of manager Bobby Robson, entered in the UEFA Cup – the first time they were in Europe for ten years. This was clearly going to be a new experience for most of the players, and the staff of the club, not to mention the suppporters who had become used to away trips to such exotic locations as Shrewsbury and Aldershot. David recalls: "People at the Club were a bit unsure as to how to deal with negotiations over travel, hotels and ticketing, and were happy to deal with people such as us at Felixstowe Travel, who had done a bit of travelling and could put them onto the type of hotels, airlines and local handling Agents they were going to need. An example was a phone call I received from the Club Secretary, Wally Gray - a lovely man, but not well travelled. 'David' he said, 'How many stars has this Hotel de Ville in Paris got?'I had to tell him gently that this was not a hotel at all, but the Town Hall of Paris where the Cup Draw was to be made.

When the draw paired Ipswich with Real Madrid – one of the greatest teams of Europe, whose home pitch was at one of the grandest stadia – the Bernabéu – on the continent, there might have been a tendency to feel over-awed. But not a bit of it – the team fought out a hard won, if slightly fortunate, victory at Portman Road (courtesy of an own-goal) in front of a 26,000 capacity crowd, and so were ready to face the howling mob of 80,000 people in the Bernabéu. The match was no great footballing feast, as Town were determined to hang on to their lead, and so they did, to win through by the narrow margin of that own goal at Portman Road. I was sitting next to the mother of Ipswich centre forward David Johnson, an excited and rather large lady, who when the final whistle blew simply gathered me up and kissed me! But these things are all in the line of duty and the trip was a very successful and enjoyable one for all who travelled."

OPPOSITE
The Ipswich party arrives at Madrid airport in 1973.

10

Second Round

24th October 1973

Ipswich Town 4   Lazio Roma 0

7th November 1973

Lazio Roma 4   Ipswich Town 2

Following a first leg 4-0 win at Portman Road, we travelled to Rome the day after Fireworks day in 1973. It is incredible to look back at the events of this match, both on and off the pitch. Nothing like this could or would happen in this day and age. The score seemed irrelevant, only that Ipswich went through 6-4 on aggregate.

Both the Lazio supporters and their team were aggressive in the extreme. The Ipswich players had never witnessed intimidation and aggression like it. Trevor Whymark, who scored four goals in the home leg, and had been fêted by Roma, Lazio's hated neighbours, was a special target. The Swedish referee was totally ineffective. The dressing room doors had to be locked for over two hours after the match to stop Lazio players and other thugs from getting in. The crowd were also hostile after the match, and several scuffles broke out.

Philip recalls – "I think I visited 12 supporters in Rome hospitals that night. None were serious. In those days there were no UEFA Officials, no TV cameras at every game. However, as a result of the behaviour of both their fans and supporters, Lazio were banned from from UEFA competition for the following season. It was a game that all who played in it and all who were there in Blue and White will never forget."

Third Round

8th November 1973

Ipswich Town 1   FC Twente Enschede 0

12th December 1973

FC Twente Enschede 1   Ipswich Town 2

We were to play FC Twente several times over the next few years. This was our first visit to Enschede, an industrial town in eastern Holland. It was easy to reach by coach, travelling via Harwich/Hook of Holland, and so a good number of Ipswich fans were in the surprisingly large crowd of 23,000. It was a two day trek for Town fans, with an overnight stay after the match. Twente had been regular players in the UEFA Cup and were to continue this run for many years to come.

Dutch fans were, in those days, notoriously

OPPOSITE
At F.C. Twente.

The Supporters Club, The Football Club and Felixstowe Travel

In the first three seasons Ipswich were in Europe, Philip was Secretary of the Supporters Club and was later to become its Chairman for the following 15 years. It was to the Supporters Club that the Football Club initially turned for guidance and it was us, as Felixstowe Travel Agency, that the Supporters Club appointed as their official travel agents – a position that was then ratified by the Cobbolds on the Board of ITFC. This was in turn agreed by UEFA who ensured that it was only we who could receive the official allocations of tickets to away games.

This meant that tickets could only be sold as part of a travel package, and did not fall into the hands of touts or known hooligans. Later stringent regulations included a Membership scheme with photo card that could be confiscated by foreign police if there was any trouble. No card – no travel.

For the Real Madrid match we chartered an aircraft at a cost of £25 a seat. The flight was shared with the players and the Press, but we ensured that the fans paid no more than the officials!

badly behaved, but the Dutch police were more concerned prior to the game, about Ipswich fans, but a large presence found they had to spend more time controlling their own fans!

Ipswich were 1-0 up from the first home leg, and goals from Peter Morris and Bryan Hamilton ensured a 3-1 aggregate win. Frans Thijssen was playing for FC Twente, and impressed Bobby Robson, who later brought him to Suffolk. On to the Quarter Finals in our first season in Europe for more than 10 years!

ABOVE
Trevor Whymark scores in penalty shoot-out in Leipzig.

Fouth Round

6th March 1974

Ipswich Town 1   Lokomotive Leipzig 0

20th March 1974

Lokomotive Leipzig 1   Ipswich Town 0

This was to be a trip to remember for the number of fans who made the long journey.

A two day tour was organised and by this time Ipswich were beginning to attract the attention of the national sporting press and broadcasting media, so the Press party included Gerry Harrison, well known as the Anglia TV commentator, but who also wrote for *The Times*, and Peter Jones the legendary BBC radio commentator (who could later forget his commentary on our FA Cup Final victory in 1978). Philip writes – "Peter was a tall, imposing and cultured figure who had that memorably unforgettable voice. He was to

die later at a regrettably young age from cancer, and was greatly missed by friends and colleagues. There has, in my view, never been a commentator like him since."

The trip for fans included a visit to the infamous Colditz Castle and nearby Brewery – we wonder how many still have the Colditz beer mugs in their kitchens?

As for the game – well Ipswich were 1-0 up from the first leg, but Leipzig were undefeated at home, and 57,000 East German fans packed their huge open bowl of a stadium. Mick Mills was sent off for retaliation, but even after extra time the tie was level at 1-1 and Town faced their first European penalty shoot-out. The East German keeper saved from Allan Hunter and Ipswich were out.

SEASON 1974–75

UEFA Cup
First Round

18th September 1974

Ipswich Town 2   Twente Enschede 2

2nd October 1974

Twente Enschede 1   Ipswich Town 1

This was to be the first time that Ipswich were to be knocked out at the first hurdle in the UEFA Cup. It was the second year in succession that we had to travel to the wet and windswept Twente stadium. Having drawn the first leg at home 2-2, it was always going to be an uphill struggle. And so it proved against the old enemy from Holland. Bryan Hamilton scored in both matches, but a goal by Bos after just 7 minutes meant that Ipswich would have to score at least twice. They didn't manage it, and so Ipswich went out on the away goals rule. Frans Thijssen again played against Town - soon he was to become an important member of Ipswich's UEFA Cup winning squad.

RIGHT
Kevin Beattie lets fly with a left foot thunderbolt.

OPPOSITE
Acknowledging the crowd. From left to right. Mick Mills, Peter Morris, Geoff Hammond, David Johnson, Trevor Wymark and Allan Hunter.

The Hooligan Problem

The problems caused by British football supporters travelling abroad had been evident for some time before Ipswich Town's second entry into Europe in the early 1970's – indeed it was not only the European grounds that were targeted but away supporters in England were enough of a problem for our Police to cope with.

There had been a number of unsavoury incidents in Europe – notably the behaviour of Leeds supporters in the aftermath of the European Cup Final in Paris in 1975…and the rioting of some 'Spurs fans following the UEFA Cup Final against Feyenoord in Rotterdam in 1974. But there had also been earlier incidents involving followers of Chelsea (Bruges 1971) and Glasgow Rangers (Barcelona 1972); and more were to follow with followers of Manchester United (St. Etienne 1977), Liverpool in Belgium (1978) and West Ham (Madrid 1980). International matches also attracted the less salubrious fans with England rioting through the streets of Copenhagen, Basle and Oslo, as well as Scottish fans on the rampage in Germany.

The growing problem was causing even the Government to give some thought to it, since the reputation of the country was being harmed. And it was also affecting us as travel organisers because we were increasingly finding that hotels were reluctant, even refusing, to take in groups of the "British hooligans". Prior to the first Ipswich Town trips to Madrid and Rome, we got together with the Football Club and agreed a series of regulations governing supporters travel. Firstly, the Club agreed that only we, Felixstowe Travel, as their official Travel Agents would be able to handle their allocation of match tickets, and they did indeed inform all opponents of this. This was important because it enabled us to ensure that virtually everyone that travelled was going to have to abide by our Code of Conduct. We were able to supply tickets to those who wanted to travel independently - for instance by car – as long as they signed an undertaking to abide by the Code. It was interesting for us to find out much later that some other clubs allowed tickets to go through many more agencies – Liverpool sometimes worked with as many as 40 travel agents .

The rest of our regulations related to the actual travel arrangements. They were as follows:

- On any official trip anyone under the age of 18 must be accompanied by a responsible adult.

- Official Ipswich Town Supporters travel cards were issued and had to be produced when booking trips. They could be confiscated in the event of the holder causing trouble.
- Banners and Flags were banned but scarves, hats and rattles were deemed acceptable
- Alcohol was not to be allowed on coaches

These rules were very well received by the FA and by the Minister of Sport, as well as getting a good reception in the National Press. Several other clubs started to follow our lead and we were asked to talk to some of them – We recall a trip to White Hart Lane where we sat in a box overlooking the pitch whilst we gave the Spurs management a run down of our ideas. The Minister of Sport – Dennis Howell – also incorporated them into a set of recommendations he issued through a Working Party on Crowd Behaviour he set up in 1975. The FA also reacted by forming an England Travel Club which took the same line as we had with our cards.

These regulations helped us considerably to ensure that the reputation of Ipswich Town supporters was the best in the country, and we were universally hailed as the best behaved of all. The national media put it all down to the country yokels from Suffolk not knowing any better, but in fact it was not simply down to the regulations, but also to the amount of detailed planning that went into every trip. This was especially true of the shorter ones to the closer countries such as Belgium and Holland, that usually involved sea and coach travel, and some quite large numbers. The essence was to see that the supporters were not left in any one place for long enough for them to consume too much alcohol. We were getting drawn to these countries quite often so we became quite practised in the art of continuous momentum – but we several times needed to charter whole ships – from either Harwich or Felixstowe for crossings that would last several hours. We sometimes had to decide whether to keep the bars on board open or shut them down. On one occasion, when we had a 6 hour daytime crossing to Europoort, in Holland, we decided to keep the bars open and found that by the time we arrived in Holland most of our people had fallen fast asleep – so that solved that problem!

In the end it was the supporters themselves who were so proud of their reputation that they ensured that there was virtually no trouble on our away Euro tours. We always produced a Newsletter for each tour, giving details of what was to be seen in the city we were visiting and including a letter from either Bobby Robson or one of the players, asking the supporters to ensure they kept the reputation of the Club intact.

FAR LEFT

As seen by Roy Ullyett in the Daily Express on 25th July 1975.

LEFT

Article taken from The East Anglian Daily Times 23rd July 1975.

SEASON 1975–76

UEFA Cup
First Round

17th September 1975
Feyenoord 1   Ipswich Town 2

1st October 1975
Ipswich Town 2   Feyenoord 0

help the friendship between the fans , which had diminished long before Whymark scored the 2nd of our away goals. There were crowds of over 30,000 at both matches.

Second Round

22nd October 1975
Ipswich Town 3   FC Bruges 0

5th November 1975
FC Bruges 4   Ipswich Town 0

A surprisingly easy 4-1 aggregate win against the most famous of all Dutch clubs, was built on a first leg away win by 2-1 with goals from Trevor Whymark and David Johnson. Feyenoord were at the time, League leaders and favourites to win the UEFA cup. Clive Woods and Whymark scored in the 2-0 home leg win.

Travel to Rotterdam was easy - we organised trips by Air, Coach, Sea and Rail. Not for the first time, we chartered one of the Sealink (now Stena Line) Ferries between Harwich and the Hook of Holland. The open stadium was not helpful in the terrible weather, and like Enschede before, the bucket seats became impossible to sit in. The situation of them - right at the front and therefore below two tiers of Dutch fans above, with various missiles pelted down on us, did not

With the home leg first, and a 3-0 lead to take to Belgium, the odds were on Ipswich progressing. But by half time, Bruges had scored three times and the tie was level. Then a fourth goal in the second half put the Belgians through in an amazing comeback from the dead. This associated Town with an unwanted record in the UEFA Cup/Europa League, best comeback, which has since been matched by a number of clubs.

Again, thousands of Town fans were given easy travel passages and cheap fares. Felixstowe to Zeebrugge was a regular ferry route then, and we chartered the whole ship to take 1,200 fans that way. Flights were also chartered, and many supporters travelled with their own cars. Bruges

is one of the most beautiful cities in Europe, and the Town fans were, as always, respectful and well behaved, though there were a few that were not. David writes – "I had formed a good relationship with the local Police Chief on my preliminary visit – he later came to Felixstowe as a guest at our Rotary club - and he told me just to stand in the Market Square and tell his officers if I needed any help. In fact a small group were playing up and clearly the worse for drink, and when I challenged them they told me in no uncertain terms that they were travelling independently and not part of any of our tours. I experienced a moment of pure power when I signalled to the nearest policemen, and the whole group were rounded up and put on the ship to be returned home without delay!"

"By chance, a few months later I was arranging for a large group of Church people from our Diocese – about 800 of them including our Bishop – to go on a day trip to Bruges on an exchange basis with the local Roman Catholic church and a service in their Cathedral. When making the arrangements with my friend the police chief he remarked how similar the planning was to the football tour. 'Oh yes,' I told him – except that the songs will be very different!"

ABOVE LEFT
Club President, Lady Blanche Cobbold often liked to travel with the fans – here she is on board the ferry from Felixstowe.

THIS PAGE
Cheering on the Blues in Belgium and Holland.

OPPOSITE TOP LEFT
George Burley evades a Feyenoord challenge.

OPPOSITE TOP RIGHT
David Johnson celebrates his goal at Feyenoord.

OPPOSITE BELOW
A desparate challenge in Bruges involving Allan Hunter.

Pre-match preparation

David remembers - To prepare for the trip I took Town Secretary David Rose with me on a preliminary visit and we found it a most civilised place. The Landskrona Chairman took us both back to his home, right by the water's edge, looking over The Sound to Denmark, and he cooked us bacon and eggs as we chatted. Their Coach was also something of a character. Finn Willy Sørensen by name – he had trained at Lilleshall, and learned most of his English there, so almost every other word was a swear word. The local reporter turned up and wanted us to pose for a photo, so there we were, David Rose, Fin Willy and myself examining the grass in the centre circle when Fin Willy proclaimed loudly – "Oh look - bird shit!"

We were told that the local supporters had a habit of forming a procession from the town centre to the stadium before each of their games, and we asked if our people could be allowed to join in. The police were aghast at the idea, but they eventually gave in and in fact our people joined several hundred of theirs on the two mile march. We were in the habit of taking a box full of Ipswich Town memorabilia – old programmes, badges, etc, for our people to give away, especially to the local children, and this had a really beneficial effect here. By the time we got to the Stadium there were hundreds of British and Swedish people, all arm in arm and singing lustily and accompanied by the local pipe band. The police chief couldn't believe his eyes! What neither of us knew at the time was that this was the same night that the notorious Manchester United mob were running riot in St. Etienne.

But the darker side emerged after the game – as we found our coaches had been broken into and a lot of items stolen, including travel documents. It meant I had a sleepless night making out lists of lost property and arranging temporary replacement passports.

SEASON 1976–77

With Town finishing 6th the previous season, there was no European football. But in this season, they came third in the First Division, and so were once more entered into the UEFA Cup for 1977–78.

SEASON 1977–78

UEFA Cup
First Round

14th September 1977
Landskrona Bois 0   Ipswich Town 1

28th Septmber 1977
Ipswich Town 5   Landskrona Bois 0

This was to be a memorable Cup season for Ipswich Town and their supporters, and at least we had some slightly more exotic destinations – with European travel to Sweden, the Canary Islands and Barcelona, and it all culminated in that fabulous FA Cup win at Wembley in May 1978.

An easy aggregate score of 6-0 against the part timers from Southern Sweden – Trevor Whymark scored four in the home leg - should have meant a pleasant journey for supporters, and indeed we could use the magnificent TOR Line ferries from Felixstowe to Gothenburg – an 18 hour journey that allowed plenty of time for drinking and carousing. But in fact our people were very well behaved and most enjoyed the good life of a cruise type ship, with the famous Swedish smorgasbord meals and good entertainment on board. We stayed in Gothenburg hotels, as there was a better selection there, and travelled by coach down the coast to the small seaside town of Landskrona, which was north of Malmo and almost opposite Copenhagen. Some of our people took the flight option into Copenhagen, though in those days before budget flights, it was an expensive option.

ABOVE
The Away programme.

Second Round

19th October 1977

Ipswich Town 1   UD Las Palmas 0

2nd November 1977

UD Las Palmas 3   Ipswich Town 3

This was a perfect draw for supporters who wanted a winter sunshine holiday, plus some football! One week tours, three day and one day trips were all organised.

David says – "The memorable thing for me was that we chartered a De Havilland Comet – the first ever jet airliner – from Dan Air, and as it was full the pilot invited me to sit in the spare crew seat on the flight deck. I shall not forget the approach to Grand Canary, with the sight of snow capped Mt Teide on Tenerife straight ahead.

The game itself was quite lively, but off the field we had an interesting trip to a barbecue restaurant that was advertising a "mock bull fight." This turned out to be a young bull tied up in a ring that was being harassed by some of the customers well charged with drink. Would our supporters be likely to turn down an opportunity of this sort? No way, but when one of them climbed into the ring and took hold of the bull's horn, it literally came off in his hand!

Ipswich went through 4-3 on aggregate, though it was touch and go after a slender 1-0 home win. But goals from Mariner (two) and Les Tibbott, secured a 3-3 draw in a picturesque stadium holding 25,000 fans.

The day prior to the game, Patrick Cobbold and Philip were walking along the promenade above the beach, followed by a contingent of journalists. Patrick was explaining to them that this (pointing to the beach) was where "These Latin Countries find their best players. Look at that bunch there – they look as if they could be half decent players," he said. One of the journalists pointed out to Mr. Patrick that they were 'his' team having a training session!

Third Round

23rd November 1977

Ipswich Town 3   FC Barcelona 0

7th December 1977

FC Barcelona 3   Ipswich Town 0

An amazing 3-0 home leg win gave Town fans plenty of hope for the second leg in spite of the opponents including Cruyff and Neeskens in both games. However a shock was in store. Although the crowd was only 24,000 in the vast – and very wet – Nou Camp stadium, the home team had obviously been threatened by manager Rinus Michels, and in a game dominated by Johan Cruyff, the score after extra time was 3-0 to Barcelona – thus 3-3 on aggregate. In the penalty shoot out, Barca miss just once, whilst Talbot, Viljoen and Woods all missed for Town.

However, it was at least another chance for town fans to get some sunshine and a few days holiday - to drown the disappointment of another UEFA Cup exit.

But never mind – there would be Cardiff, Hartlepool and Bristol Rovers still to visit in the first three months of 1978 – all of course in the FA Cup – and who will forget the Semi Final against West Bromwich at Highbury, and the fabulous final at Wembley against Arsenal – which one national paper headlined as "The One Nil Slaughter." Those were indeed the days.

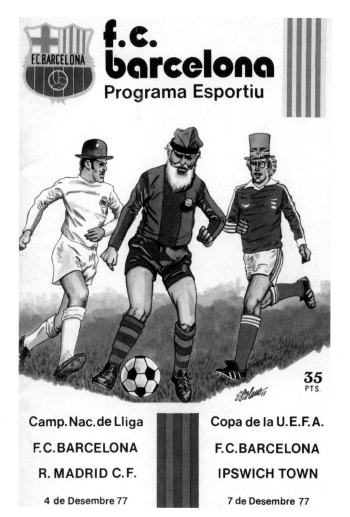

ABOVE
Barcelona issued one programme for two games – they had played Real Madrid just before us.

27

SEASON 1978–79

Cup Winners Cup
First Round

13th September 1978

AZ Alkmaar 0   Ipswich Town 0

27th September 1978

Ipswich Town 2   AZ Alkmaar 0

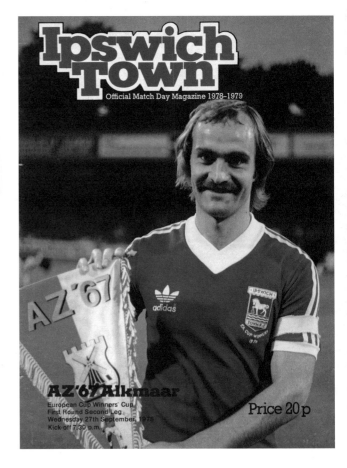

Having won the FA cup at Wembley in May 1978, Ipswich Town were entered in the European Cup Winners Cup for the following season.

Destined to meet a year and a half later in the UEFA Cup Final, Alkmaar were Ipswich's first opponents in the Cup Winners Cup competition.

Drawn away first, Town fans travelled to the beautiful small town in northern Holland, more famous for its cheese production than football. Again we had the problem of a lot of people wanting to travel, and cheap costs making that possible. We were able to charter a whole ship from Felixstowe for the six hours crossing to Europoort, near Rotterdam, so our coaches had an easy journey to the stadium and we could also bring them back by overnight crossing without having to arrange accommodation.

Says David – "On my preliminary inspection visit, I was rather alarmed to find that there was no form of segregation within the stadium to keep rival supporters apart, and also the local Police told me they did not operate inside the stadium but left security there to the Club's own stewards.

OPPOSITE
Kevin Beattie tries a header in Alkmaar while Mick Mills (no 7) and Trevor Whymark look on.

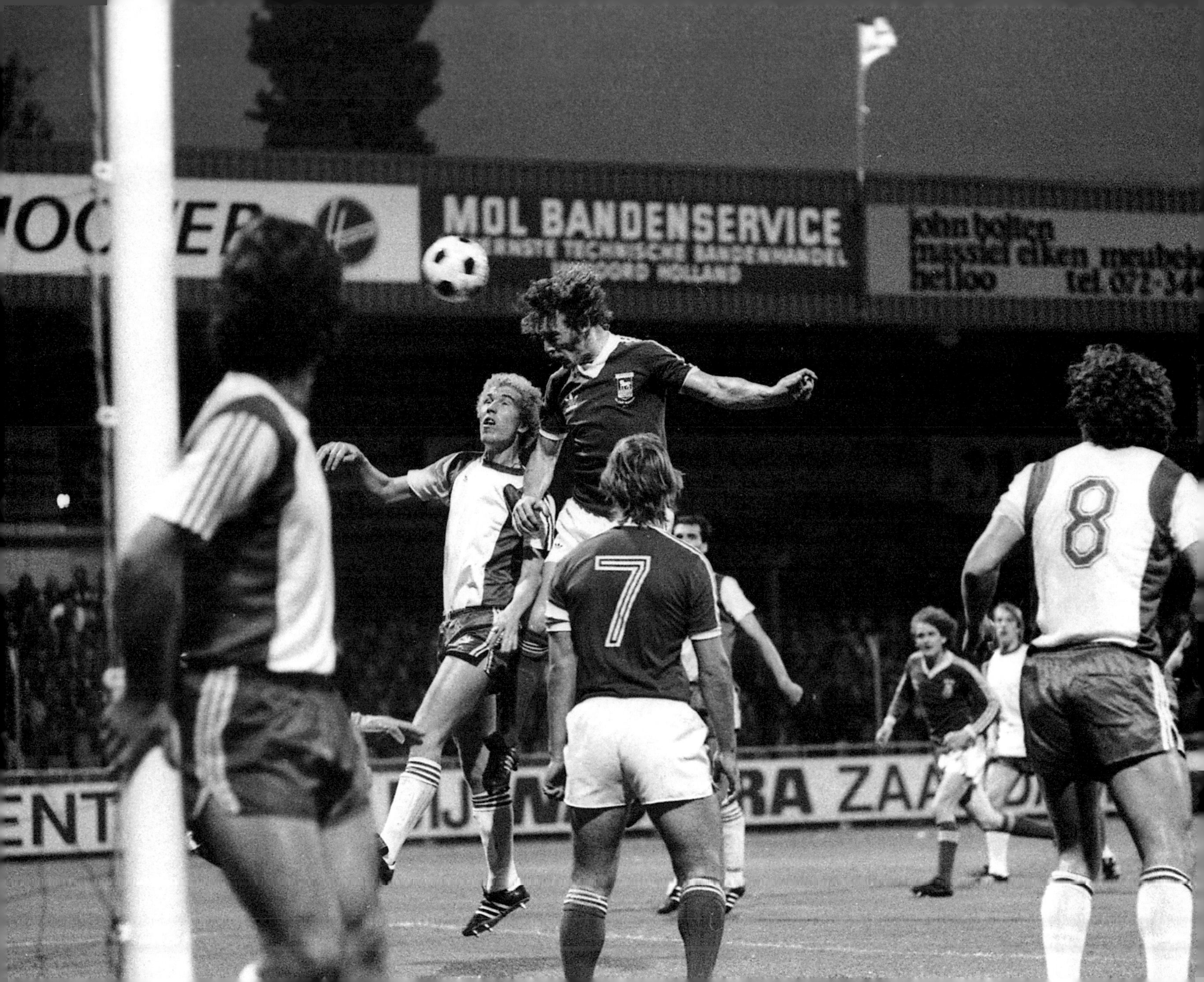
MOL BANDENSERVICE
john bollen

As Ipswich were due to play Manchester United at Portman Road the following week, I invited the Alkmaar General Manager to come and see what security our club had in place for that. He and one or two of his colleagues did just that, and went back and built some fences in their stadium!

In fact this was a clockwork operation a far as we were concerned. The timings we worked out meant that coaches could stop two or three times in Holland for refreshment, but not for long enough to consume more than one drink. I told the Alkmaar police what time they would arrive in the town, and sceptical though they were I noticed that they were quite impressed when the first of our coaches loomed over the horizon at the exact time I said they would!

IPSWICH TOWN FOOTBALL CLUB CO. LTD.

REGISTERED OFFICE PORTMAN ROAD IPSWICH IP1 2DA ENGLAND   TELEPHONE IPSWICH 51306 AND 57107

Directors
Patrick M Cobbold (Chairman)
K H Brightwell
John C Cobbold
W Kerr
J M Sangster
H R Smith

Manager
R W Robson
Secretary
D C Rose

Colours Royal Blue/White
V.A.T. Registration Number
102 3660 20
Company Registration Number
315421 England

Members of
The Football Association
Suffolk County Football Assn
The Football League
The Football Combination
Mercia Youth League
South East Counties League

Honours
Football League Div 1 Champions
1961-62
Division 2 Champions
1960-61 1967-68
Division 3 South Champions
1953-54 1956-57
FA Youth Cup Winners
1972-73 1974-75

I am pleased to be able to write a few words to the Ipswich supporters heading for Holland and our European Cup Winners' Cup game against AZ '67 Alkmaar.

It goes without saying that we look to each and every one of you to preserve the good name of Ipswich Town by being on your very best behaviour throughout the trip. By all means cheer as loud as you can but remember the serious consequences that crowd disorder can bring.

We go into the match at Alkmaar knowing quite a bit about them having met them in the final of the four club tournament at Bruges last month. On that occasion we lost 2-0 but we were under strength due to injuries and I am looking for more from this match.

Alkmaar will provide us with stiff opposition, of course, but we have a good track record in Europe and have no need to fear them. They are one of Holland's up and coming sides and in last season's UEFA Cup were knocked out by Barcelona after a penalty decider. I need not remind supporters that this was exactly what happened to us in the next round.

Over the years we have forged a close friendship with several Dutch clubs. Apart from our European matches against FC Twente and Feyenoord, we have met several others in pre-season games, including NAC Breda, Go Ahead Eagles and Utrecht.

I sincerely hope that you all have an enjoyable trip and that we give you plenty to cheer about on the way home. Remember you are all ambassadors for Ipswich Town...

Bobby Robson

A small crowd of 10,000 saw a goalless draw, although Mariner had a goal disallowed and Kees Kist hit the bar for the Dutch.

As to the security within the ground, this consisted mainly of stewards with dogs leaping up against the wire fencing in front of our people. They were very soon quietened down, however, as our people took great delight in feeding them (the dogs, not the stewards!) hot dogs through the wire netting! The game was being shown on live TV in Holland and the audience must have been told how good the Ipswich supporters were being, because as we drove our coaches in convoy out of the town after the game, a large number of residents came to their doors and waved us goodbye. This was probably the most emotional moment I had in the whole of my football experience."

This draw kept Town's unbeaten run on Dutch soil going a little longer. The home leg resulted in a 2-0 win for Ipswich, with goals from Mariner and Wark.

LEFT
Alkmaar 1978 – Bobby Robson's appeal to the suporters.

1

3

5

2

4

Second Round

18th October 1978

Ipswich Town 1   SW Innsbruck 0

1st November 1978

SW Innsbruck 1   Ipswich Town 1

Third Round

7th March 1978

Ipswich Town 2   FC Barcelona 1

21st March 1978

FC Barcelona 1   Ipswich Town 0

1-0 up from the first leg, Ipswich travelled to the picturesque alpine ski town of Innsbruck. A breaking of the curfew at the team hotel led to local journalists writing headlines in the Star of "Bad Boys in Blue." A stormy tie goes into extra time, when George Burley nets the equaliser on the night and sends Town through 2-1 on aggregate. Burley is injured by a bad tackle as he scored, and earlier Paul Mariner is sent off for time wasting.

Philip recalls – "I was commentating with Pete Barraclough for Radio Orwell and Mariner was caught offside. No one could hear the Ref's whistle in the din of that small ground, including Mariner himself, who ran on and netted the ball. It was a second yellow for Town's striker."

For the first leg at home, Eric Gates replaced the suspended Paul Mariner – and scored two goals, but Barca got an invaluable away goal through Esteban. The Spanish team infuriated the Town fans with their rugged tackles, and cushions rained down onto the pitch. So for the second successive season, Town travelled to the Nou Camp this time to face 100,000 Barca fans. Despite huge pressure, Town restricted the Spanish Cup Winners to a single goal – but lose on away goals.

1 *Mick Mills exchanges pennants.*
2 *Mick Mills heads the ball.*
3 *Fans at Innsbruck.*
4 *Alan Brazil in action.*
5 *Paul Cooper being carried off injured by Cyril Lea.*

OPPOSITE
Alan Brazil heads at the Nou Camp.

ABOVE
Paul Cooper pulls off a spectacular save vs. Grasshoppers in Zurich.

BELOW
Terry Butcher kicks at the Nou Camp.

SEASON 1979–80

UEFA Cup
First Round

19th September 1979
Skeid Oslo 1   Ipswich Town 3

3rd October 1979
Ipswich Town 7   Skeid Oslo 0

Second Round

24th October 1979
Grasshoppers Zurich 0   Ipswich Town 0

7th November 1979
Ipswich Town 1   Grasshoppers Zurich 1

Back to the UEFA Cup again for Ipswich, and a trip to Norway for Town fans, who got a shock at the price of food and drink – the tax on alcohol there is huge! The small stadium held only 3,000 fans, and it was an easy 3-1 win for Town, with goals from Mills, Turner and Mariner. The Team stayed in an ultra modern City centre hotel, and the journalists were joined by John Motson on the day of the game. A keen fan of the Club, John was not often seen at away European matches, usually having to commentate on the European Cup (now Champions League) matches.

The home leg was a walk-over with Town scoring seven goals, and eventually winning by the aggregate score of 10-1. Memories of Malta over 15 years earlier!

A surprising 0-0 draw, although the Swiss side contained seven Internationals and were top of their League at the time. Supporters travelled in numbers yet again, and in spite of high hotel prices, a three-day air tour and a virtually non stop coach trip were also arranged.

Philip recalls – "I will never forget the face of the manager of the 5 star hotel, where the Team and the fans on their chartered air trip were staying – when into the luxurious hotel foyer burst over 100 Ipswich fans from their coaches, singing and shouting 'Give us an I...' with flags and scarves waving aloft."

The home leg looked over when Kevin Beattie scored just before half time, but a late goal from Sulser gave the Swiss an aggregate win on away goals.

SEASON 1980–1981

**UEFA Cup
First Round**

17th September 1980
Ipswich Town 5   Aris Salonika 1

1st October 1980
Aris Salonika 3   Ipswich Town 1

The long, historic UEFA Cup winning campaign starts against difficult Greek opponents. However a 5-1 home leg win sets up a comfortable second away leg.

Not too comfortable for the Town fans, however. At the training session the night before the game, Ipswich fans were attacked and the team bus was stoned. Local and National journalists were amongst those forced to run from the stadium under a hail of stones. This incident made headlines on all back pages in the UK next day, and the Aris fans were probably the most aggressive we ever met on our European travels. Even the team needed a police escort to get them out of the stadium after the game.

Many fans opted for the 'holiday' option of the many tours offered. Staying at holiday resorts

on the Halkidiki Peninsular, near Salonika, the weather was excellent and the holiday interrupted only by the small matter of a UEFA Cup match!

With Salonika 3-0 up with 25 minutes left, Town were grateful for their four goal home lead – but an away goal at Portman Road meant the Greeks needed only one more goal to go through. Enter Eric Gates, and his first shot hits the back of the net. Town are through 6-4 on aggregate.

ABOVE
The Stadium at Salonika.

37

Second Round

22nd October 1980

Ipswich Town 3   Bohemians 0

5th November 1980

Bohemians 2   Ipswich Town 0

The first leg at Portman Road was won 3-0 by Town. Second half goals – two from Johnny Wark and the other from his replacement Kevin Beattie, set up what should have been a comfortable second leg. However in sub-zero temperatures an injury weakened Town side conceded an early goal. Beattie, in his trademark short sleeved shirt was a master of the defence. Robin Turner hit a post and then Bohemians score again. Town hold out for the last 40 minutes, and scrape through 3-2 on aggregate.

David recalls – "This was without doubt the coldest weather I have ever encountered at a football game. I did my best to dress for the match – pyjama trousers under normal ones, two pairs of socks, two sweaters – with a wad of the newspaper type programmes they produced, fed in between them. We had a mass undressing session at the airport afterwards – I had hitched a lift back on the team plane, which was enlivened by Allan Hunter donning a stewardess' hat and apron and handing round the drinks. Driving back through Ipswich at around 3am was the only time I have ever been stopped and breathalysed. I was well inside the limit – but only because the stewardess service on the flight had been so slow!"

Third Round

28th November 1980

Ipswich Town 5   Widzew Lódź 0

10th December 1980

Widzew Lódź 1   Ipswich Town 0

Manchester United and Juventus had already lost to this strong Polish team, but Ipswich brushed them aside in the first leg home game. Scoring five goals (including a hat trick from John Wark) for the second time this campaign, they conceded just one in the second leg. However the game was played in terrible conditions, and on a bone hard frozen pitch. As well as the freezing temperatures, the political situation in Poland had put the match in some doubt. Town played out a low key game and lost by one late goal. The journey back to the airport was rather fraught in the heavy snow – in fact the van carrying the team kit went off the road twice.

Fourth Round

4th March 1981

St. Etienne 1   Ipswich Town 4

18th March 1981

Ipswich Town 3   St. Etienne 1

This date, March 4th 1981, and this game will go down in the annals of Ipswich Town history. St. Etienne were the team of Europe, the UEFA Cup favourites and French League favourites for the Championship. Their team included stars such as Michel Platini, Johnny Rep, Battiston, and Paganelli. A daunting task, then for Ipswich. The supporters came in their thousands by land, sea and air. At the end of the game, they couldn't believe what they had just witnessed. This was, without doubt the best ever Ipswich Town display by a country mile.

Johnny Rep headed the home side into an early lead. But Ipswich hit back ten minutes later. Mariner heads home the equaliser at the far post, then Muhren powers in a long range shot straight from the second half kick off. Butcher's shot is half saved and Mariner puts in the rebound. On 76 minutes, John Wark headed in Town's fourth, and his 30th goal of the season. At last the national Press, next day, gave Ipswich the credit they deserved and they were now a European team to be respected.

The second leg was played at Portman Road on March 18th, in front of a capacity crowd. Kevin Steggles is given his Town debut. The President of St. Etienne proclaimed Ipswich as the best team they had ever played against. Some praise!

The Town team didn't just sit back – they went out and annihilated the French masters for the second time in two weeks, winning 3-1 with goals from Butcher, Wark and Mariner. Not for the first time in this memorable season, Ipswich were in a

ABOVE
Terry Butcher in action at St. Etienne.

cup semi final – the FA Cup Semi Final against Manchester City was due to be played just three days after the UEFA Cup Semi Final first leg. These were breath-taking days indeed!

Kevin Steggles remembers this match for a different reason. He was in Italy with the Town's youth team, playing in a tournament there, when he got the call to join up with the first team party. He flew from Pisa to Lyon in the company of "Mr John" (Cobbold) but in the event didn't even get on the bench. However, he made his first team debut a fortnight later in the home leg of the tie.

Philip writes: "When I look back at this match, and indeed this period in time, I don't think many Ipswich fans realised how lucky they were, nor how good the team was.

We were not to know that this decade was to become the Club's 'Golden Period', and that there was not going to be another for at least 20 years. At the time, we just took it for granted that Ipswich were going to be in Europe every season, and that we, the fans, would rarely experience the bitter taste of defeat in League, Cup or European games, for year after year.

Maybe, if we had known what the next decades would bring, we would have savoured every match, every high, so much more. I know I would have."

> **UEFA Cup Semi Final**
>
> *8th April 1981*
> **Ipswich Town 1   FC Cologne 0**
>
> *22nd April 1981*
> **FC Cologne 0   Ipswich Town 1**

At this time both the Semi Final and Final were played on a home and away, two leg basis.

Being drawn away in the first leg would seem to give the Germans a slight mental advantage, but it didn't turn out that way. Cologne had the former Nottingham Forest and England star Tony Woodcock playing up front, and they also boasted German international stars such as Littbarski in midfield, and Schumacher in goal.

A tense game finished 1-0 to Ipswich thanks to a John Wark goal after 34 minutes.

A great save by Paul Cooper kept out a fine shot by Littbarski.

And so to the away leg. At Felixstowe Travel we were inundated with ticket requests from British Army forces serving in Germany, as well as thousands who wanted to make their own way there. We were a little worried about the Army presence, although we were assured by senior officers there would be a strong Military Police

OPPOSITE
Paul Mariner shoots as Terry Butcher looks on at St. Etienne.

RIGHT
In the Mungersdorfer Stadion.

presence. As it turned out, although the soldiers had a strong hatred of everything German, and their behaviour was certainly worse than any Town supporters had shown before, there were no ugly incidents.

David says – "I was staying in a hotel in the central square of the city opposite the Cathedral, and looking out of my window on the morning of the match I saw two groups of supporters – one group wearing red favours, the other in blue – haranguing each other in the square below. It was looking as if it might get nasty, so I thought

43

I had better go and see if I could sort things out. It was only when I got very close to the altercation that I realised that both groups were shouting in German. I have no idea who they were, but I withdrew quite quickly. Later in the morning, the German Police chief I had contact with rang me to ask if I could identify a certain English man, whom he named. I said he was not known to me and was not travelling on one of our tours. It transpired that this unfortunate man had disembarked, totally drunk, from a train in Cologne station and crashed through the plate glass window of a shop. He was supposed to be en route for quite another occasion in Munich!"

Town had lost their FA Cup semi final, and were playing their third game in a few days. The home game ended 1-0 to Ipswich with a goal from Johnny Wark. In the second leg with 55,000 people in their magnificent stadium, Terry Butcher was to head in the winner in the 64th minute. The photo of Bobby Robson and Bobby Ferguson dancing a jig of joy on the touchline is an iconic image of this amazing season.

So, Ipswich win the tie 2-0 on aggregate, and here we were, in our first European Final.

David recalls: "The feeling was a little unreal, until – while sipping a beer quietly afterwards,

Philip and I suddenly realised that we had just two weeks before the first leg of the Final, in which to set up and organise travel arrangements for the thousands who would want to be there. We knew later that night that our opponents were going to be our old friends AZ Alkmaar, so we set off at dawn by car from Cologne to reach Alkmaar and re-introduce ourselves to their management. But they told us as soon as we arrived that they had decided that their Stadium was going to be much too small for such a momentous night in their history, so they had switched their leg of the Final to the Olympic Stadium in Amsterdam. At least we knew we should not have any trouble getting enough tickets. To say that the next two weeks were going to be hectic would have been the understatement of the century!"

Philip writes: "My memory of Cologne is of a long, long coach journey, and seeing at last the Stadium across the parkland. As we walked through the park approaching the impressive Stadium, there was Town Chairman, Patrick Cobbold waiting to greet all the fans with a smile, a handshake, and a quip."

The UEFA Cup Final

UEFA Cup Final 2 Legs
First leg
6th May 1981
Ipswich Town 3   AZ Alkmaar 0
Second leg
20th May 1981
A Z Alkmaar 4   Ipswich Town 2

In the first leg, Eric Gates' early challenge on an Alkmaar striker might have given the Dutch a penalty, but that was the nearest they were to come to a goal. Hovenkamp handled to give Wark yet another penalty, then Thijssen scores straight from the second half kick off, and Paul Mariner heads Town's third on the hour.

Philip recalls. "I remember the days leading up to this match, as I was appointed the Agent to the Dutch team. I organised their training schedules, booked them into the Orwell Hotel in Felixstowe, and took their manager to Middlesbrough the previous week to watch the game against Ipswich. Ipswich had to win, and Aston Villa lose for Ipswich to become League Champions. Unfortunately neither happened. The Dutch team

trained at Felixstowe Town's home ground, in Dellwood Avenue, and watched Ipswich Town match videos. Ipswich loaned them the use of their new Team coach for the duration of their stay."

The second leg was played, not at Alkmaar's picturesque, but small home ground, but at the Olympic Stadium in Amsterdam, which was also the home ground for Ajax. However the crowd of 28,500 (7,000 of whom were Ipswich fans) didn't

ABOVE AND PAGE 46
Fans in central Amsterdam.

PAGE 47
Every vantage point taken in the Olympic Stadium.

PAGE 48
Kees Tol scores for AZ.

PAGE 49
Butcher heads, while Thijssen, Tol and Wark look on.

continued on page 51

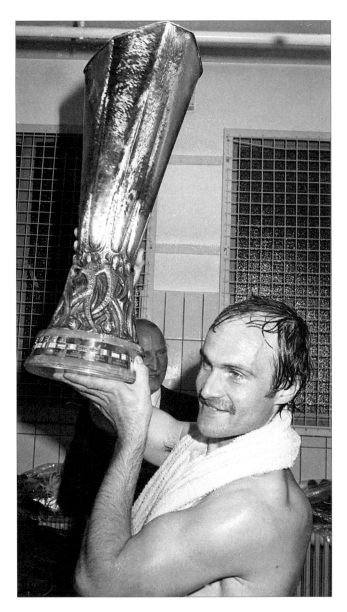

really justify that decision. For our supporters, it was of course a dream come true. Amsterdam was at the time one of the most accessible of any of the European capitals, with ferry connections from Felixstowe and Harwich and flights from Norwich, Stansted, and Cambridge. We could offer a plethora of official tours from which to choose, whether for one day, two days or three day tours by air and sea, and of course thousands making their own way by car.

Planes were chartered, ferries were chartered and seats block booked on scheduled flights from all airports. We managed to find around 50 coaches to hire. This was to be the largest exodus of Ipswich Town supporters to an away European match. We took altogether around 5,500 people. In spite of a local transport strike in Amsterdam, the huge operation of moving these numbers of football supporters went without a hitch.

David recalls: "Part of my brief was to stay behind after an operation such as this in order to sweep up any supporters who had been detained either in a hospital bed or a police cell, but when I entered the office of the Commissioner, he said to me 'Mr Houseley, I have never seen anything like this in 35 years of Police service.' I wondered what was coming next ... 'We had no problems.

OPPOSITE
A Dutch celebration on the Amsterdam pitch, as Arnold Muhren and Frans Thijssen run with Town fans and the media.

LEFT
Mick Mills raises the cup again, this time in the dressing room.

No incidents – oh yes, I forget, there was one problem – one of your people was bitten by one of our police dogs. But it was the fault of the dog and the handler. We made sure he was treated properly and put him back on his correct coach.'

It was indeed an organisational triumph, and I was proud of the way we had dealt with the smallest detail – for instance I had to remember that a lady on coach 34 was in a wheelchair and I had to obtain a pass for her to the disabled area of the stadium.

Once inside the stadium I saw there was a fight going on between supporters at the opposite end to where our people were supposed to be. The local stewards however, told me not to worry –they were Ajax and Alkmaar fans, who hated each other at any time, just taking the opportunity for a set-to!"

The match itself was a cliff hanger, despite Town's 3-0 first leg lead. The good weather had continued, but it was Alkmaar that turned up the heat with a display that belied their first leg performance. Welzl, Metgod and Peters are dominant in midfield. At half time, Alkmaar lead 3-2 but still trail by two goals overall.

Thijssen and Wark had scored the first half goals. Jonker scored another for Alkmaar in the 73rd minute, but Ipswich hang on in a tremendous finale. Ipswich won on aggregate 5-4 and one complete end of the Olympic Stadium – bedecked already in Blue and White, went crazy. It was a magical moment, and not one of the Ipswich fans who were there will ever forget that day.

Philip writes: "The 1,000 or so fans who travelled on the chartered ship from Harwich to the Hook of Holland, were under the Stewardship of myself and Richard Powell, together with a few police officers. We experienced no trouble at all, even when we decided to close the bar for a few hours before we docked. And no trouble after the match, when those fans were delayed by a coach drivers strike. This meant that the 20 coaches were late arriving at the Stadium, and 1,000 fans were left standing in a vulnerable spot. Again no problems ensued, and Richard and I were on the last coach to leave Amsterdam. Arriving at The Hook late, the Ferry was about to depart, and when Richard and I had ensured no one had been left behind, the ship was actually moving away from the dockside, and the vehicle ramp was going up. We had to make a leap of faith to get aboard!"

Celebrations

Philip writes: "This was the third major Cornhill 'homecoming' I had attended. This was far better attended than the Championship reception in 1962, and far more colourful and noisy than the FA Cup celebrations three years earlier."

The Cornhill and the area around was just a sea of Blue and White. Fans were on the lamp-posts, on the roofs of Lloyds bank, the Post Office, Grimwades, Mannings pub, and every vantage point was taken. The Cornhill was just a waving, singing and swaying mass of joy. When the open top bus swung round from Princes Street onto the Cornhill , you could see the look of total astonishment on the faces of the players, as they took in the unbelievable scene. When Bobby Robson and the players eventually came onto the Town Hall balcony, it took an age before they could make themselves heard, even with a sound system. It was to be a never-to-be-forgotten occasion for all those fans who were there.

LEFT
Bobby Robson leaves the Town Hall with the silverware.

AFTER THE EUPHORIA...

Season 1981–82

**UEFA Cup
First Round**

16th September 1981
Ipswich Town 1   Aberdeen 1

30th September 1981
Aberdeen 3   Ipswich Town 1

Ipswich were in Europe for the ninth time in ten seasons, by dint of finishing second to Aston Villa in the league table. But the evidence of a downward trend was clear – and the all-conquering, Cup winning team was beginning to break up. Bobby Robson was also continually being linked to each and every managerial vacancy that arose. The Aberdeen tie was in fact to be Robson's last European involvement with Ipswich Town as he was to take up the post of England Manager soon afterwards.

We chartered a train for the lengthy and rather miserable journey north- with entertainment on board, and there were also charter flights from Norwich airport only to see our team outplayed by one man in particular – Gordon Strachan - and out-manoeuvred by their Manager – Alex

Ferguson, two men whose influence on the game was to last for many years ahead, as of course was Bobby Robson – this was indeed a meeting of the great and the good!

Ferguson had assembled a fine team which, apart from Strachan, included Jim Leighton in goal, plus star names such as Rougvie, McLeish and Weir. The first leg at Portman Road had ended in a 1-1 draw with Frans Thijssen scoring a trademark goal – dancing past defenders before lashing a fine shot into the net.

The match itself was disappointing. Wark fouled Strachan in the box and the little man himself scored from the spot. Then Gates was brought down in the home area, and Wark scores to equalise. However, Aberdeen's record signing Weir, got two great goals. Paul Cooper saved a late Strachan penalty, but Town were beaten 2-4 on aggregate and were deservedly out at the first hurdle.

Philip writes: "The charter train was something of a throwback to the 1960's, when the Supporters Club chartered trains regularly to away League games. Then called the 'Blue Arrow', the trains had an intercom system for Quizzes, often a Disco and other entertainment. Together with Richard Powell, who was involved in the original

"Blue Arrows" with Tommy Parker, we tried to replicate those special trips. We organised plenty of entertainment on the outward journey, and the time passed quickly. The return journey was mostly spent sleeping!"

Season 1982–83

UEFA Cup
First Round

15th September 1982
AS Roma 3 Ipswich Town 0

29th Setember 1982
Ipswich Town 3 AS Roma 1

Our second visit to the Olympic Stadium in Rome was nowhere near as exciting as the first – the notorious battle against Lazio in 1973 – had been. The stadium was still largely uncovered but the match attracted a lively crowd of some 60,000. Ipswich were now under the managership of Bobby Ferguson but his team never looked like upsetting the Roma pedigree performance in this electric atmosphere, and they saw a brilliant display of attacking football from their team. This was a display Paul Cooper would want to forget,

and the Turkish referee disallowed a Paul Mariner strike for handball.

In the home match we saw a far better Town performance and at one time they looked as if they might pull it off, with Gates, McCall and Butcher scoring for Town, but Maldera got the all-important away goal to put them through. In the end we went out by 3-4. At least the Ipswich Town in Europe saga was to end – as it turned out for almost 20 years – on something of a high.

Keith May from Southwold recalls: "One of my regular visits to Rome on behalf of the Ministry of Defence for discussions with the Italian Air Ministry coincided with the Town's UEFA Cup away match with AS Roma in September 1982. Over lunch on the day before the match, when I mentioned my Ipswich connections, an Italian colonel asked if I'd be attending. No, I said, I hadn't planned to. The following morning he presented me with a ticket for the match, and wouldn't accept any payment.

When I got to the stadium I found that I was not in the 'visitors' section of the crowd, but amongst the Roma fans! I was made to feel very welcome and at the final whistle I was escorted by four of their fans, safely to a nearby bus stop."

A NEW ERA DAWNS...

There followed a period in the wilderness for Ipswich, as a succession of managers attempted to bring them back into what had become the Premiership. After Bobby Ferguson, there came John Duncan, John Lyall, and Mick McGiven. And then came George Burley, who wanted to recreate, as manager, the good times he had experienced as a Town player. He masterminded Town's promotion to the Premiership and in their first season , they finished 5th – and were unlucky not to have come at least third, just three points behind Champions League qualifiers Liverpool.

Season 2001–02

**UEFA Cup
First Round**

20th September 2001
Ipswich Town 1 Torpedo Moscow 1

27th September 2001
Torpedo Moscow 1 Ipswich Town 2

Almost 20 years after their last European game, Ipswich Town - now under the managership of George Burley, who had been named Manager of the Year for his first season in the Premiership,

were drawn against the crack Russian team. The first leg, at home, was shown live by the BBC.

Torpedo went ahead in the first 15 minutes and only a very late equaliser by Titus Bramble gave Ipswich hope for the second leg and preserved Town's unbeaten home record in Europe.

Philip writes: "At this time, as well as being Chairman of the Supporters Club, I was also Press officer on match days, together with Geoff Dodson. At the press conference at the end of the home tie – during a period when Ipswich were winning regularly – there was a lull in questions from the journalists. From the back of the room, I asked George: 'Do you ever look at the fixture list and wonder where the next defeat is coming from?' This caused hilarity in the packed room, and George smiled broadly! We have beeen good friends ever since. As we talked earlier about Gordon Strachan and his impact on Ipswich when we were knockled out of Europe by Aberdeen some 20 years earlier, I remember taking him, with Geoff Dodson on the long walk from the Dressing Room to the Media Centre. Always a joker, he said, half way, 'I don't go this far on holiday!'"

The crowd in Moscow was a paltry 7,000 with just a few fans making it from Suffolk. An early open goal missed by Torpedo gave Ipswich confidence and Venus' corner found George, who fired home. In the 54th minute, that same player won a penalty which Marcus Stewart converted – making amends for his first leg miss. Ipswich were now in command and lead the tie by two goals, but a well-offside goal by Vyasmikin is allowed to stand and Town had to hold on for the remaining 25 minutes to go through on a 3-2 aggregate.

Red Square was a focal point for Ipswich fans before the match and the Russian Police and Secret Service were out in force. But of course, there was never going to be any trouble. Richard Powell was walking through Red Square with a friend who was smoking a cigarette. Many fans had earlier received on the spot fines for smoking in Red Square (Apparently against the law, but no signs to that effect). Richard and his friend were stopped by the Police who wanted to see their passports. However they received a smile, but no fine. Richard puts this down to the fact that they were staying at the Radisson Hotel (the best in town at that time), who had put stickers on to their passports, and the police had been impressed and decided not to impose any fine.

Second Round

18th October 2001

Ipswich Town 0   FC Helsingborgs 0

1st November 2001

FC Helsingborgs 1   Ipswich Town 3

In the home leg, Town found the well organised Swedes a hard nut to crack and only Town's Italian goalkeeper, Matteo Sereni kept Town level.

2,500 Ipswich fans make the trip to the attractive port of Helsingborg, which has strong connections with Felixstowe. They had an early shock in the small stadium when Sereni allowed a shot from Eklund to slip through his hands. But after the break, Town are dominant, and superb crosses from Mark Venus allow Hreidarsson, with a volley, and Stewart, with his head, to put them ahead. Marcus Stewart completed the scoring with a delicate chip, so Ipswich won 3-1 on aggregate.

Philip writes: "It was a good experience for Town fans, albeit an expensive one.

For a start, the majority of fans were on an open terrace behind one of the goals, in the old, traditional way of enjoying football.

I travelled with a friend who had a shipping business at the Port of Felixstowe, and who did a lot of business with the port of Helsingborg. We were not alone – a surprising number of supporters/shipping agents took the opportunity of meeting their Swedish customers. The team and the Press were staying in an ultra-modern hotel in the town centre, where the prices at the bar were astronomical. John Motson, who was commentating on the match for the BBC, arrived and was warmly greeted by the Ipswich Directors. A few local bars did good business after the match, in spite of the prices. I guess a lot of the customers there from Suffolk were on expenses! Many fans stayed in Copenhagen, where costs were a lot lower, and they used the ferry between the cities to get to and from the match."

Third Round

22nd November 2001

Ipswich Town 1   Inter Milan 0

6th December 2001

Inter Milan 4   Ipswch Town 1

Town thought they deserved an easier draw after getting this far in the competition, and keeping a clean sheet and getting a first leg lead, had put their supporters in a fine mood. Sereni had to

Season 2002–03

UEFA Cup
Qualifying Round

15th August 2002
FC Avenir Beggen 0   Ipswich Town 1

29th August 2002
Ipswich town 8   FC Avenir Beggen 0

ABOVE
San Siro Stadium.
OPPOSITE
Back row (left to right) – Clapham, Marshall, D.Bent, Miller, Gaardsøe, Venus; Front row (left to right) – Richards, Stewart, Wilnis, Wright, Armstrong.

make several great saves, and Bramble managed to miss a cast iron chance. Town played Sixto Peralta against his former club, but it was Alun Armstrong who came on as a sub, though not fully fit, who nodded in a Clapham cross in the 81st minute to give them the advantage.

8,000 Ipswich fans invaded the San Siro – 40 years after they had last played there - but the huge stadium was strangely lacking in atmosphere with only a total of 26,000 there and Ipswich could not repeat their record of away wins for the previous two rounds. The technically superior Italians ran riot with four goals and though Town got a late Armstrong penalty they lost out 4-2 on aggregate.

Ipswich Town were surprised to find themselves back in European competition, despite having finished only 18th in the Premiership. This was down to the Fair Play League – in which UEFA added up all the red and yellow cards awarded against the many clubs and gave a UEFA Cup place to those with the smallest number.

However, they had to go through the qualifying round to get the first of what turned out to be three trips to some remote places in the far corners of Europe. The part timers from Luxembourg put up a stout show before a crowd of under 3,000, the majority of whom were from Suffolk - they held out until injury time when a goal from Marcus Stewart gave Town an away goal advantage. They hardly needed that for the second leg when they scored no less than eight times, including a hat

trick from Pablo Counago. A goal-fest indeed but the biggest cheer of the night was for the attractive lady physio of Beggen who, judging by her smile, took the adulation in the spirit it was intended!

First Round Proper

19th September 2002
Ipswich Town 1   FK Sartid (Smederevo) 1
3rd October 2002
FK Sartid (Smederevo) 0   Ipswich Town 1

"Where on earth is that?" was the question first asked. Actually Smederevo is in Serbia, part of the former Yugoslavia. Having allowed the opposition to get ahead after just 30 minutes, in the home leg, Town were a bit fortunate to get an equaliser ten minutes into the second half.

The second leg saw Town take a lucky lead when Marcus Bent was pushed in the area and converted the penalty himself. Town had complaints about racist chants from Sartid supporters, as well as time-wasting tactics from their team, but were glad to get home with a 2-1 result under their belts.

Second Round

31st October 2002
Ipswich Town 1   Slovan Liberec 0

14th November 2002
Slovan Liberec 1   Ipswich Town 0

In the few short weeks since the last round, George Burley has been sacked and Joe Royle appointed in his place. The home leg was rather fraught, with the Czechs hitting the woodwork twice before Darren Bent scores his first ever European goal to give Town a fragile lead.

Liberec was eventually to be found on a map of the Czech Republic, some way north of Prague, and the team were reputed to be a hard side to beat at home. They scored a late goal to bring the tie into a penalty shoot-out. Matt Holland and Darren Bent both score, but Jermaine Wright and Finidi George have their shots saved. Slovan scored four of theirs so Ipswich go out – out of Europe, but for how long?

OPPOSITE
Cheers in Luxembourg.
LEFT
Under surveillance in Smederevo.

THE MEN THAT
MATTERED
Bobby Ferguson remembers...

Bobby Ferguson joined the Ipswich coaching staff in the early1970's, becoming first team coach, and then taking over as Manager in 1982 when Bobby Robson left to take up the post of England Manager.

Here, he recalls the qualities of some of the characters who were the backbone of that Cup-winning team, and some of the events that stand out in his memory.

Arnold Muhren

When we were looking for a left sided midfield player, we asked agents, and our contacts in Europe to tell us who they thought was the best. All of them said Arnold Muhren.

And they were right! We played him on the left and we played him in the middle. Variation was our secret weapon, and opponents were totally confused – none of them could handle Arnold Muhren.

He was not a physical player – when we played Barcelona, for instance, we were a bit worried about Arnold as he was going to be marked by Neeskens, and he didn't like tough tacklers. However in the event he played well and it wasn't a problem.

Frans Thijssen

We asked Arnold to recommend a right sided midfielder, and he immediately said 'Frans Thijssen – he's a better player than I am!' When we signed him, Bobby Robson put him in the reserves and he was just outstanding. Beating four or five players with ease, and showing such class. When Bobby asked me if he was ready for the first team, I had no hesitation in saying 'Yes'. He was simply brilliant.

But we wanted to get him to pass the ball more, especially when someone like George Burley was making a run down the wing. He was too often waiting for a pass from Frans that never came. On one occasion we made the point again. Right from the kick off, Frans beat four or five defenders including the Keeper, then just passed the ball into the empty net. As he ran past me on the bench, he said 'Well, I did pass it, boss!'

When, after the 1978 FA Cup Final, we sold Brian Talbot to Arsenal, and then bought Arnold and Frans with the proceeds –and we still had money left over. That must have been one of the best bits of business the Club ever did!

Alan Brazil & Eric Gates

We preferred to play Eric Gates behind the two strikers – Alan Brazil and Paul Mariner, from where he would ghost into scoring positions, but could also score from range.

If this didn't work, and we were chasing the game, we put Eric in the Box, and played Brazil wide. Otherwise the box would get too congested. We liked to vary our play so our opponents were confused. But Alan, great striker as he was, didn't like playing wide.

He wanted to score goals, and of course, we wanted that too, but it didn't always work out that way and we sometimes needed to change tactics during a game. While Gates liked to receive balls at his feet, Brazil liked the ball over his shoulder, and playing wide was against his natural instinct, but for the greater good of the team, we needed to do this occasionally. Alan and I often were at loggerheads over this tactic.

Johnny Wark

Johnny's eye for a goal was unique for a so-called defensive midfielder. His coolness from the penalty spot a was also a great asset to us at vital times.

Mick Mills

Mick was a calm and assured captain, who had command on the ball, and was quick to pick up on any change of tactics and why they were necessary – not all players are able to do that. He was a leader in every sense.

George Burley

I worked with George from the age of fourteen and a half, until he left the Club, and can honestly say that he was a pleasure to work with, in as much as his attitude to hard work and the development of his skills. He developed a range of passing, short and long, to great effect and was very quick to see a break from defence to attack – his forays down the wing were his trademark, arms flying and often followed by an accurate cross into the box.

It was great blow to us when he was injured at Shrewsbury, and was unable to take part in the second half of the UEFA Cup run.

Allan Hunter

Allan was really important in his role at centre-half – he really was at the heart of the defence. When Butcher, Osman and Beattie came in to make their debuts, he was the father figure on the pitch at vital times in their careers.

Terry Butcher

Terry was another extremely good user of the ball, especially with his left foot. He had a great defensive brain and could play very well at left back – which in itself speaks volumes for his ability when you realise that he was 6'4".

Russell Osman

He was well balanced, and completely two-footed – I never knew which was his best foot, and neither did he! He was just about our toughest tackler.

Kevin Beattie

An absolute natural with his pace and power in the air - he did not need much coaching. I remember when I first played him, in the youth side at Cambridge – we needed a centre-forward for that game so I pushed Kevin up there. He scored six goals in a 6-0 victory. I'm sure their keeper was diving to get out of the way of some of Kevin's left foot blasts !

Paul Cooper

A very under-rated goalkeeper, and for a long time he was the only internationally uncapped player in our team. He had very good hands and saved us on numerous occasions with his uncanny ability to save penalty kicks. He would have been an even better goalkeeper in today's game as he was a skilled player with the ball at his feet. He originally started his career as a centre-forward and had great pace off the mark in sprints. Balls played back to goal would never be a problem for Paul.

Paul Mariner

I regarded Paul as the kingpin of the Gates, Brazil, Mariner strike formation.

He was a born leader of the line. Strong in the

air, a good team player, and a big motivator of the rest of the players. His hold up play was excellent, and that was vital against big, strong centre-halves, and his lay-offs and distribution were always good. A big player for the big occasion, he was a very important part of our success in those glory years.

Steve McCall

During the European campaign of 1980/81, George Burley suffered a serious injury that was to force him to miss nearly half the season and much of the following season. In Steve McCall we had a perfect team player.

He was predominately left footed, so we switched Mick Mills to right back, and put Steve at left back. I nicknamed him "Sticky", because once he had the ball, it was virtually impossible to dispossess him. He rarely gave the ball away, was a great distributor, a strong tackler and a very reliable player. He came into the team at an important time in the season, when every match was a big game, and he stood up to be counted, and never let us down.

Sizing up the Opposition

I was usually the one appointed to go on the advance trip to see what kind of opponents we were going to have to face, and these trips were usually instructive, sometimes pleasant - and sometimes not.

St. Etienne

I went to watch St. Etienne in a league match, and when I got back, Bobby Robson asked me what we were going to do about Platini. "Nothing," I said. "If he plays deep, then Wark can pick him up. If he plays forward, then Osman can mark him." Yes, I think it was one of our best performances. We silenced the Green Hell, as their fans were called. They were notorious and could intimidate opposing players. But we kept them quiet early on. We played our short game, kept Platini in check and it worked like a dream.

Salonika

The advance trip did not prepare me for the horrendous atmosphere we experienced from their crowd at the match. The Referee was clearly terrified of the crowd. We cleared three of their efforts off the line, but the Ref gave them three goals! But finally Gates scored a goal from 25 yards to ensure we went through. After the game their supporters threw flints at us as we boarded the coach. They were sharpened and made holes in the bodywork. If they had hit anyone, they would have been badly cut. It was the worst crowd we have played in front of since the Lazio game.

Widzew Lódź

Again I went over a week in advance to watch them play. It was freezing, there was a lack of food, and the town was really rough. There was clearly a lot of poverty, but the people could not have been friendlier. I had an Interpreter, who asked me if I could bring him back an E.L.O. record. When I returned with the team, we stayed in Warsaw, and when I saw the Interpreter, he was so pleased with the record, he kissed my shoes! The pitch was snow covered, but had been rolled flat. It was very icy. The game went ahead, but on the way back, Trevor Kirton our Kit man, who was driving a van with the kit inside, when he skidded off the road, and turned over. He was picked up by a group of

Hungarian musicians and only just made it back to the airport in time for the flight.

Often on these Eastern European trips, we did take our own food and chef with us – mostly cereal and steaks.

Ipswich Town supporters

The Club and the Players always appreciated the support they received from the fans. At home matches they created a fantastic atmosphere. And we knew on away European matches that there would be no trouble, even if they were taunted by opposing fans. We really appreciated the away following all over Europe, and we always knew where our fans were situated as they always made themselves heard, and that was wonderful.

On becoming Manager

I was invited to become Manager after Bobby Robson left to take over at the FA, as Manager of England. My first and only UEFA Cup match in charge was against Roma, where we lost 3-4 on aggregate.

However, at the beginning of the next season, our Chairman, John Cobbold, told me we had to sell players because of the financial state of the Club. As a result of the building of the Pioneer (now Britannia) stand, there was a huge debt, and the Club's bankers were not being helpful. I was told I had to raise £500,000 before August, so that the Club could meet the debt re-payments. Not only did I have to sell Alan Brazil to Spurs, eventually I sold no less than 22 players – many of them Internationals. So, we went into Europe that year with kids playing in the first team, and thus had very little chance of progressing.

GOLDEN MEMORIES...

Memories of 'Mister John'

Chairman of Ipswich Town 1957–1976

David writes: The memories of John Cobbold, Chairman of Ipswich Town from 1957 until 1976, when he was succeeded by his brother, Patrick, are many and varied , perhaps best related by Mel Henderson in his biographical book, "Mr John".

He was a famous *bon viveur* and most of the stories seem to revolve around drinks of one kind or another, but he also had a great sense of humour and was a practical joker of the highest order. One of my favourite tales was when the Club installed a grand and expensive new astroturf surface in the indoor training area, and the Press and local great and good were invited to its unveiling. Just before they were due, John went out and bought a bag full of mushrooms which he planted strategically among the "grasses". The ensuing chaos can only be imagined.

John was a plain speaker in a strong way. I recall that we were in the boardroom at Portman Road, awaiting the arrival of the official party from St. Etienne to discuss arrangements for the matches with them. They were late, and John was becoming irritated at the delay, when he called out at the top of his rather loud voice " Where the hell are those f…..ing froggies." They were in fact just coming up the stairs and must have heard him, so we just had to hope that their English was not ,shall we say, up to the colloquial! At any event they made no sign that they had understood him, and relations between the two clubs were excellent – indeed the President of St. Etienne said later that Ipswich were the best team they had played against.

Both the Cobbold brothers several times made it clear to us how much they appreciated the reputation for good behaviour among the supporters that we had helped to establish, and we knew we always had their support. This was crucial in the beginning when we needed to establish ourselves as the official travel agents to the Club and the only avenue through which supporters could obtain tickets for the away games.

But my abiding memory of John will always be the time when I had checked them into the Hilton Hotel in Amsterdam, and seen them up to their rooms. Half an hour or so later I was still at the reception desk, sorting out rooming lists, when out of the lift came John. "Ah, David", he said – "I've drunk half the contents of my mini bar - how do I get it refurbished?" "I'll sort it in a few minutes, John" I said, "but what about the other half?" "Don't drink minerals," came the riposte.

Pat Godbold

Pat was an Ipswich Town supporter for nine years prior to her appointment in 1954 as Scott Duncan's secretary. Bobby Robson described her as a loyal and faithful servant of the Club. She is now the Club's Archivist.

Pat's memories of European trips.

Milan 1962

When we landed at Milan's airport, the plane taxied to a halt a few hundred yards from the Terminal, for some reason. It was pouring with rain, but airport officials were at the bottom of the steps with large umbrellas, to escort us to the Terminal. I had a seat high up in the huge stadium, the biggest I had ever been to. The atmosphere was strange, because it was les than half full. Ted Phillips, who wasn't playing because of injury, saw me at half time, and beckoned me down to sit next to him, behind the dug-out.

Milan 2001

I travelled on a 'day' trip – 24 hours from Ipswich back to Ipswich! We left at 5am with hundreds of Town fans for the air tour. When we arrived in Milan, the airport looked a little different from almost 40 years earlier! We were taken to the

City centre for some sightseeing and shopping. Then the 56 coaches had a police escort direct to the stadium, with crossroads closed, giving us a non stop journey. The stadium had changed a lot as well! It appeared that the seat numbers on the tickets meant nothing - it was a case of sit where you can. They didn't have Stewards, as we know them, nor even police inside the Stadium. Just soldiers with guns!

The UEFA Cup Final

Mr. Robson said I could go on any of the tours I wanted to, at the Club's expense. Being a thrifty person, and not wanting to waste the Club's money, I chose the cheapest Tour. Coach and Ferry, via Sheerness to Flushing. Mr. Robson's brothers were on the same trip. After the match, we went back to the players hotel, and it was a late night! We almost missed the ferry the next day. And we were welcomed back at Sheerness by over-zealous Customs officials, who virtually stripped every coach in a search for drugs. Of course they found nothing. The Football Club's President - Lady Blanche Cobbold - went by Air on a one day tour.

She was in her 80's at the time. Mr. Patrick gave her the use of his room at his hotel, so she could rest before the match.

It was a memorable game and a memorable occasion. I believe over 7,000 of our supporters were there, and there was no trouble and no arrests.

Interestingly, the Football Club received many letters, including from the Captain of the St. George saying it was an amazing return journey, made enjoyable by the well behaved Ipswich supporters, who were a credit to their Club, and to football. Another letter came from an elderly couple who were travelling on another ferry, and were warned that hundreds of Ipswich fans would also be on board, and did they wish to change their reservation. They decided not to, and wrote to say what a wonderful journey they had experienced with the humorous and well behaved Ipswich fans. A letter from the Commissioner of Police of Amsterdam also complimented the Ipswich fans for their behaviour.

Aberdeen 1981

I flew from Southend to Aberdeen, and on arrival at the airport, heard a voice calling me. It was Jimmy Leadbetter's daughter! She said he would be at the game and that we should have dinner with them afterwards. It was good to see Jimmy and his wife and daughter after so many years.

Pat Edwards and Jill Lewis

Pat Edwards has been a Town supporter since 1962, and helped form the Clacton Branch in 1969, becoming Secretary soon after. Jill Lewis joined Pat on the Clacton committee and the two have been inseparable travelling companions ever since.

Their memories include the following.

Our first trip into Europe was to Twente Enschede in 1974. We flew from Southend airport to Rotterdam in an old propeller driven Macedonian Aviation DC3, and repeated the experience the following year when we played at Feyenoord. We, too, recall the less than friendly Feyenoord supporters who pelted us with all kinds of missiles from above when David Johnson scored the winning goal from a Clive Woods cross. We had to put cardboard boxes over our heads, and it was very scary!

But that was forgotten when we went to Landskrona in Sweden. We had a 22 hours crossing from Felixstowe to Gothenburg aboard the "Tor Britannia" and among our fellow travellers were Paul Cooper's Dad and Betty Felgate, the "Supporter of the Year" – for that year and many others. Lots of people will remember Betty, who was one of the most loyal of supporters.

ABOVE
Jill Lewis.
BELOW
Pat Edwards.

We have lovely memories of meeting with the Landskrona supporters in the city centre and then walking arm in arm with them to the football stadium with a pipe band leading us. There was no mention of this great atmosphere in the papers next day – the Press were only full of the Manchester United hooligans abroad! They did not want to report on the good things about football.

We travelled home on the "Tor Scandinavia" in a Force nine gale. The sea was so rough that all the crockery was smashed in the restaurant, and we had to use paper plates. Quite a few people had minor injuries after falling from one side of the ship to the other. The football was excellent, but our coaches were broken into and bags and passports stolen.

Our first experience of Eastern Europe came in 1980, when we were drawn against Bohemians of Prague. There was a six day coach and sea tour, in some very cold weather, and after staying a night or two in Nuremburg, we well remember crossing the "Iron Curtain" and the scary looking border guards with guns. When we stopped in Pilzen - famous for its lager – to get some fuel and change money, our drivers, Chris and Jim, were fined twice for parking in the wrong place. The fines

were £3 and £8 which I suppose was quite a lot of money in those days, but the atmosphere was dreary as it was still ruled by the Russians. There were armed solders and tanks on the streets, red flags on all the pubic buildings, and very little in the shops, but Jarmila, our Czech Courier, said she would "rather be red than dead!"

There were several "ladies of the night" frequenting our hotel lobby, and they got one of our supporters so drunk he passed out, and they made off with his wallet, so he missed the match!

We were sittting with some local supporters at the game and they were eating some form of sausage that they offered to share with us. It tasted frankly awful, but we felt we had to reciprocate and as we had some Cadbury's chocolate we offered them some. They went quite mad about it and insisted on giving us all of their sausage in exchange for all of our chocolate. Not a fair exchange, we thought, but in the spirit of international relations we let them get away with it. It was all done in sign language, of course, but in football terms that can count for a lot!

We stayed in Prague again 22 years later, in November 2002 when we played Slovan Liberec, and the atmosphere was completely different, though we did still have a riot squad at the match!

1981 was certainly our greatest year as supporters as it was of course the year we finally won the UEFA Cup! For the Semi-Final in Cologne, we took one of Geoff Dodson's "Weekender" tours and stopped off in Luxembourg before going on to Bernkastel on the Mosel, with a great evening out at the Wine Village in Koblenz, where the Rhine and Mosel meet. We travelled in from there to the Mungersdorfer Stadium for the match, where the atmosphere was amazing!

For the Final in Amsterdam we again took one of the Weekender tours and had a short tour of Rotterdam before going on to the pottery at Delft, and Scheveningen (try and pronounce that!) Harbour before staying overnight at Noordwijk by the sea. We also had a visit to Volendam, where Arnold Muhren was born and everyone we met claimed to live next door to him! Visits to the clog makers and a cheese farm came before a tour of Amsterdam, meeting up with many of our fellow supporters on Dam Square and sampling the essential canal trip before going on to the Olympic Stadium for the match. It was an experience we shall never forget.

We ought to mention at this point that we took a "Super Sail" from Felixstowe on the Viking Viscount in aid of Allan Hunter's Testimonial, when the whole ship was chartered by his testimonial committee. Allan was on board and we had our photos taken with the UEFA Cup, so that made a perfect climax to the greatest time in our club's history – well, so far!

The years following that final in Amsterdam were to be honest a bit of an anti-climax, but in 1981 we were drawn against Aberdeen and as that was somewhere we had not seen before, we took a three day trip with Eastern National, along with Mum (Granny Aggro!) and Betty Felgate, amongst others. Staying overnight in Edinburgh enabled us to see the Castle, Holyrood Palace and Arthur's Seat. We remember crossing the Forth Bridge and visiting Pitlochry and Braemar on Royal Deeside, passing close to Balmoral Castle. These football trips do get you around - but unfortunately, we lost 3-1 to Alex Ferguson's team and it was a very long overnight journey home, arriving back in Ipswich at 12 noon the next day.

In 2001 we went to Moscow, another new experience for us. On take-off from Stansted airport in an Aeroflot UN86, the plane shook horrendously and the noise was unbearable – so we wondered what we were in for. Inside the plane, the headrest came off and some of the seats were broken , and the food wasn't very good, so we

ABOVE
Outside the stadium in Moscow.

ABOVE RIGHT
Geoff Dodson (Chairman of the Colne Valley Branch of the Supporters Club) organised special 'Weekender' tours for his members.

re-christened the airline Aeroflop!

But once we got there, we were really surprised by our magnificent hotel - the Ukraina. It was one of the Seven Sisters buildings in Moscow and was very impressive. However they wouldn't serve us any food late in the evening, and also ran out of glasses, so we were reduced to the emergency supplies we had brought with us, and had our drinks out of ice-cream sundae glasses. After a mediocre breakfast at the hotel we were relieved to find a McDonalds close to Red Square. We had to be very careful of the street urchins trying very hard to rob us – one of them was actually hanging onto the arm of Jim (Pat's husband) and trying to get his hand in his pockets, whilst another tried to get into my handbag. But we did get our

fur hats and had our photos taken wearing them in Red Square, and then we were interviewed at the stadium by Ian Winter from "Look East" and on the BBC News he said we were Clacton's answer to the Beverley Sisters! This particular snippet was later put onto an Ipswich video.

We had an early departure next morning and two members of our group overslept and missed the flight. One had fallen asleep with his bath running and flooded the room. He was arrested and as his visa only lasted a few days his had run out, it took them three days to get home by a circuitous route.

Our final trip – so far – was to Yugoslavia in October 2002. At least it used to be Yugoslavia , but now it's in Serbia. We were to play F K Sartid, in a rather depressing place called Smederevo. We stayed in Zagreb, which is in Croatia, but Jill was on a day trip and, travelling by coach to Belgrade, they were running late and the driver was stopped for speeding. However, the policeman accepted that they were going to be late for the match and signed the driver's tachograph to explain the reason. I doubt if our police would be so lenient! On arriving at the ground with the River Danube in the background, there was a sign that said, in English – "Welcome to Blue Hell!", and our seats were in "Death 98 Row". All presumably designed to intimidate us – and the ladies' loos there were no actual toilets so we had to "spend a penny" in sand and dirt!

So altogether our support for our favourite team has taken us to all parts of Europe and we have seen some wonderful sights as well as the football. We did not get to some places in the earlier years because the flights were so expensive – that was long before the days of Ryanair and EasyJet, which enable so many more people to get to the games. But we had some wonderful times. And above all we travelled in the company of a lot of lovely people – as of course all the Ipswich supporters are! We very much hope that we may have some more exotic places to visit following our team in the years to come!

Tony Scarff

Tony Scarff acted as a steward and courier on a number of European excursions over several seasons. Here he describes some of his most memorable moments.

I think it was on the way to the match against Twente Enschede, and David had gone ahead of the main group and was to meet us on the outskirts of the town to direct us to the ground. There were around 18 coaches travelling in convoy and I was appointed to take charge of the leading one.

We had not long disembarked from the ferry at Zeebrugge and were well on the way along the Belgian motorway when I was told there was an urgent need among a large number of people for a loo stop. Clearly a lot of people had taken in a lot of liquid refreshment on the ship and failed to relieve themselves before going ashore. So we had no alternative but to pull in at the next layby – which was nowhere near big enough to

take all our coaches. But there we stopped whilst a hundred or so people relieved themselves in the ditch alongside, doing a fine imitation of the famous Belgian statue "Manneken Pis!"

But suddenly there was a sounding of sirens and flashing blue lights. The leading police motor cyclist pulled up alongside us, furiously wagging his finger, and shouting "No piss on the motorway!" How you are supposed to stop a hundred or more males in full flow we didn't know – or even try, but we were soon back on our way and then had an escort of police outriders as far as the Dutch border, making sure we didn't repeat the exercise!

I also recall a similar experience with a police escort following a match at Feyenoord in Rotterdam.

We had played in a pre-season tournament, and Town had got to the final, which went into extra time. It was going to be touch and go whether we would make the port before the ship left for Felixstowe, so we enlisted the advice of the policeman in charge. The effect was dramatic – a fleet of motor cycles arrived and whilst some took the lead others roared ahead stopping the traffic at all the junctions and waving us through red lights a-plenty. It was a great feeling being treated like VIPs - the coach drivers certainly enjoyed the experience – and we did make the ship on time – just!

On another occasion I was asked to take charge of a flight to Munich when we were playing at Innsbruck. The flight arrived OK but our baggage didn't. After a long wait I went to the reception desk, which was unmanned, so I picked up a phone and dialled the information desk. The lady at the other end seemed not at all concerned and suggested the luggage might have been sent to Frankfurt or just may not have been put on the plane at all. She even suggested we could pick it up on our return journey. I told her this was not good enough, and said that our passengers were beginning to get a little irate, and that as they were British football supporters, if she didn't want to incite a riot, it might be a good idea to get some action. At this, she became a little more co-operative and assured me she would get the luggage to us as quickly as she could. I had no alternative but to accept this so off we went to Innsbruck and as we sat down to dinner at our hotel, the manager came and told us that the bags had just arrived – by taxi!

David adds: There were occasions when we used the record of British football supporters, and the

OPPOSITE
Fans on their way to Alkmaar.

bad name they had throughout Europe, to see that we got priority treatment, even though our own reputation was excellent. I recall one occasion coming into Luton airport, the Customs people looked as if they were about to put us through a thorough check, when I suggested quietly to those at the front to start singing, "Bobby Robson's Blue and White Army." The noise was tremendous, and the Customs men couldn't get rid of us fast enough!

Ian Hunneybell

A fan who kept a travelogue of the European away games in 2001 and 2002. Here are several extracts, with some of his photos.

Moscow

I was fortunate enough to have air miles and hotel points from various business trips and so was able to fly BA to Moscow and stay in a Marriott hotel – it took away some of the apprehension of travelling to Moscow. I arrived at Sheremetyevo airport and negotiated a taxi to the hotel, where I asked about any concerts at the Bolshoi and was told that Swan Lake was being shown that evening, and I had about an hour to get there. So I dashed out of the hotel and used the Moscow subway for the first time. Hardly anyone spoke English, the signs were all in Cyrillic, and I hadn't felt so out of my depth for years! Following my nose, I managed to make my way there, collected my ticket, and within two hours of leaving Moscow airport I found myself sitting in the Bolshoi, about to watch a ballet performance!

The following day I did some sightseeing, as I was now an expert on the subway, and I visited Moscow State University, saw where the ground was for the game that evening, and walked across Red Square, something my dad would never have considered during his days in the Navy when this was the heart of enemy country!

I met with fellow Town fans who came out on the day of the game, and despite warnings to the contrary, we met and drank beers with Torpedo Moscow fans, trading scarves and badges (On each of these trips I took Ipswich memorabilia specifically for trading with locals).

And so to the game. The stadium was hugely impressive, but disappointingly empty. Town played well and when we took the lead we started dreaming of our next destination! At one point, Torpedo missed an open goal and at that point I thought that luck was on our side and that we should progress. 2-1 up, late in the game, with the Russians needing two goals, I still hoped we would win since a win abroad is a very rare beast indeed. Of course, we did win, and several of us decamped to the massive Rossiya Hotel on Red Square to celebrate until about 5am! We even brought a young Russian lady back to the hotel with her five year old son, as they were a bit hesitant at the aggresion of the local fans after the game. She and her son were very pleased at being rescued by her English knights in shining blue shirts!

I stayed on in Moscow until the Sunday following the game, and took in more sights around the city and beyond. Friends of mine had business contacts in Moscow (not in the Abramovich league, I hasten to add!) and they sent a driver to take me around on the Saturday. We visited an amazing graveyard with statues to many notable Russians, including astronauts, military men, and even pets of famous people!

It was a hugely memorable trip.

Helsingborg

Drawn against Helsingborgs in the next round, out came the atlas again, and friends and I soon came to the conclusion that we could base ourselves in Copenhagen and make our way to Helsingor and take a ferry across to Helsingborg on the day of the game. The internet was proving useful for ferry timetables although I still relied on trips to Stanfords in Covent Garden for obtaining maps.

Several people, including Jon Craig who was at the time the Chairman of the North West branch of the Supporters Club and who would also be on all six European trips in 2001 and 2002, took a train to Helsingor and crossed to Sweden without a hitch. We were hugely impressed with the friendliness of the Danes and Swedes, and encountered so many Town fans in Helsingborg that we wondered where all the locals had gone. We found a bar close to the ground where we shared beer and stories with home fans, and traded yet more scarves and hats! Ipswich's good name had travelled ahead of us, and we all did our bit to make sure that good name continued.

The game was another wonderful occasion, giving us a few nervous moments but ending in another great win on the road, and everyone left the ground knowing we would have yet another chance to journey across Europe with the club.

We celebrated in Helsingborg after the game, and around midnight took a ferry back to Denmark. I remember being hugely impressed that this service was still running, reflecting that it wouldn't have been that good in England!

Once back in Helsingor, however, there were no trains, and so several of us took two taxis all the way back to Copenhagen. To this day I can't remember how far it was, how long it took or how much it cost. But it was worth it, whatever the answers to those questions!

Jon and I spent an enjoyable few days in Copenhagen, saw the little mermaid and other landmarks, and enjoyed the food and beer that the Danish capital had to offer. And so another, different but equally wonderful, trip came to an end.

Milan

The draw against Inter Milan was both good and bad. We had a chance to pit our team against one of Europe's finest, to have a wonderful European night at home - and what a night it proved to be! - and to have a trip to a great Italian city, knowing that it might be our last trip of the season. Flights and hotels were easier to organise for this trip, and it proved to be a wonderful opportunity for so many Town fans to experience supporting their team overseas.

I travelled again ahead of the game, and allowed myself a few days break. I flew to Malpensa and took the train, found my hotel and enjoyed a quiet drink, before being joined later in the day by fellow Town fans. I went to La Scala, the opera house, to see whether there were any performances during my time there, after the success of the Moscow experience, but it was the opening weekend of the opera season and tickets were so expensive I could have bought the Town squad for the amount they were asking! So, on this occasion, I had to concentrate on the architecture and the football.

I ate and drank well in Milan. I had been there on business a year earlier and so knew a couple of places. We also visited the Duomo cathedral and scaled its heights. The game itself was a different experience. The police presence was far greater than at previous games and having made our way to the suburb where the San Siro is located, we found no places to socialise and were marshalled to the ground by the police, where our bags were searched and what drinks we had were disposed. Not as friendly as the other grounds we'd visited. Inside, it was magnificent. Somewhere most of us had only ever seen on TV. And our team were about to play here! I thoroughly enjoyed the game, and we had our chance in the first half when Richard Naylor was through on his own. It was a shame the Milanese didn't show their support but there was no questioning the away support! It was very much appreciated when David Sheepshanks came and showed his appreciation to the fans while we were kept in after the game.

Despite losing, I was very pleased to have been able to go to all three away games, and to have been able to experience what so many Town fans

in the sixties, seventies and eighties had sampled. I felt very privileged.

The Town travelling shirt

As our European tour took shape in 2001 I bought letters for ironing onto my Town shirt, and proceeded to record the names of our destinations on the back - first Moscow, then Helsingborg, then Milan! When our tour ended my shirt was looking half empty and when trips to various big cities in the Premier League beckoned, especially Liverpool, I thought the shirt looked a bit arrogant, so I looked at the likely destinations the following season and chose the smallest place I could find - Gillingham - and had their name added underneath Milan! The Liverpool fans in particular, on that last day of the 2001/2002 season at Anfield, appreciated the self-deprecating humour!

Beggen

Despite relegation, we knew we had finished high enough in the fair play League to stand a small chance of a place in the UEFA Cup the following season and Jon Craig telephoned me excitedly one June or July evening saying he'd been listening to the draw on the radio in some foreign language

and thought he'd heard the name of Ipswich mentioned. Sure enough, we had been lucky enough to have another chance in Europe!

The tie in Luxembourg saw us play away first, and gave me a chance to visit another country with Ipswich. Again, I went for a few days, and had a lovely time walking though a pretty city on a sunny August day. There were so many Town fans in the main square and everyone was having a lovely time and the locals were so pleased to see friendly English fans. I had walked to the ground earlier in the day and taken photographs, etc, before returning for the game later in the day.

I'll skip over the game a bit because you will have many recollections of this. What made the trip exciting for Jon Craig and myself is that we were staying until the Sunday, and decided to travel, on the Friday after the game, out to Beggen to see where the team we had played the night before hailed from. We took a bus out of the city and found a delightful village with one of the most picturesque grounds I have ever seen, with a wood along one side of the ground. Beautiful, and again I felt privileged to see a sight that not too many Town fans would have seen.

Having the weekend ahead of ourselves, we decided to see if we could get to see another game, and we managed to find a Bundesliga game on the Saturday, in Kaiserslautern, only three train rides away! We travelled on the Saturday, across the border into Germany, not knowing whether there would be any tickets available at the ground, but fortune favours the brave and we got to the ground and there were a small number of tickets remaining, in an otherwise full ground on the opening day of the new season. It was reminiscent of a Liverpool derby, with the home team having their own Kop, and even singing 'You'll Never Walk Alone' before the game.

We had a great time, and made our way back to Luxembourg. We were soothing on a park bench in the sunshine on the Sunday when I telephoned my aunt, who had made use of my ticket at Portman Road the previous day and had seen Town beat Leicester 6-1! Never mind, we had had an exciting few days ourselves.

Smederevo

This was another of those destinations that appealed to me. The 'easy' ones I could visit anytime - Madrid, Berlin, Amsterdam etc. I enjoyed being drawn against teams from places off the beaten track, places I might not otherwise visit, and Smederevo ticked that particular box! I remember having a little bit of trouble finding it on a map, and in those days the few internet sites that could help out were written in Serbian which wasn't much help!

"Those days!" - I make it sound like bygone times, and it was only few short years ago!

My next door neighbour had a 1970s travel/ history book about Yugoslavia, and I enjoyed reading it, especially the chapter which spoke of Smederevo and its castle and its heyday in the 1500s! Also of interest to me was the recent past, and the troubles in the region, and I was very much looking forward to it. I arranged my own travel once more, at least as far as Belgrade, and this time left it to friends to book the hotel there,

for that seemed the best place to be based, and also a minibus to take a few of us to Smederevo on the day of the game.

I remember walking the streets of Belgrade with interest, seeing still the signs of damage from NATO air strikes on some of the government buildings, and walking around the Kalmegdan, the fortress on the banks of the Danube. It was all fascinating, especially all of the old military equipment including tanks that made an effective open air museum within the walls of the fortress.

The hotel we were staying in was at the bottom end of the comfort scale, and after a couple of nights I decided I wasn't going to stay there for the third night of the stay, and so I set myself the task of finding better accommodation - easier said than done! In the end I telephoned England and managed to secure a room at the Hyatt, one of the few reasonable hotels in the city. In fact, it turned out to be luxurious. I had been rooming with Jon Craig, and said that I would happily cover the cost of the room for the two of us if he would buy dinner at the hotel. It was a deal we both readily agreed to!

The hotel had spa and massage facilities and I took full advantage of all they had to offer. I still recall chatting with the masseuse who was Serbian and who told me how the war had been the fault of the aggressive Croats. I found this interesting as my doctor in the UK, a Croat, had previously told me that it had all been the fault of the aggressive Serbs!

On the day of the game we had an interesting journey to Smederevo, our minibus driver ominously bringing a map with him. I felt that I knew the way better than he did, having studied all the maps I could before going to Serbia! Credit where it's due, and he got us to Smederevo and to the motel we been told to go to in order to get tickets for the game - oh yes, we left England without tickets since SARTID had not brought them to England when they came for the first leg, and we were assured there would be no issue getting them in Serbia. As it was, we reached the motel only to find that nobody there seemed to know anything about tickets for the game, and we were instead directed to the Hotel Smederevo, and so our goose-chase resumed. Imagine our thoughts when we reached the concrete shell of an obviously defunct hotel! We decided just to make our way to the ground to see what the situation was there, and outside we found the UEFA representative, a happy, smiling bear of a man, who said we could get tickets on the door, or something

similar. Ticket situation resolved, Jon and I went for a wander all around the ground and found that it wasn't entirely completed, with metal poles protruding from bare concrete blocks at one end.

Jon and I found a small bar where we each had a pre-match beer, and I also sampled the local firewater, plum brandy. Phew - it warmed the parts that the beer couldn't reach!

There was a good following from the UK, and once again David Sheepshanks came and spoke with the visiting support, which was appreciated, as always. For the third time on these recent travels we came, we won and we left, happy knowing that our European adventure was set to continue.

Slovan Liberec

Once again we were drawn away from home in the second leg and this suited me well since it meant that the tie would be decided on the night in Liberec, making for a more exciting evening all round. Once again, I went for a few days to help soften the blow should we lose - travelling so far and then coming straight back after the game would leave no time to explore the area, and makes for an expensive and miserable trip if we get knocked out.

This tie had an extra twist for me, since my holiday year at work followed the calendar year, and – not expecting to either get into Europe or do so well – I had exhausted almost all my days on the trip to Serbia. I asked at work whether they would allow me to take a couple of days unpaid leave but as my boss wasn't a "football man" he didn't understand the importance of what I was asking and declined. This left me with a dilemma. I thought about it long and hard and decided that these opportunities to travel the continent and watch your team don't come along very often - in fact there was, and still is, the possibility that it would never happen again in my lifetime. I decided, therefore, to resign! I wrote out my letter of resignation, and had it in my jacket pocket as I went to work, that day in October 2002. Fate is a wonderful thing, and before I had the chance to deliver my letter news broke that the company was going to be restructuring and there was a strong chance I would be a casualty. Rather than being devastating news, I kept my letter in my pocket and sure enough, I was one of those whose services were no longer required and I was sent on 'gardening leave' – never has a man been so happy to be told he is not needed! So this solved my dilemma and I went ahead and booked the trip.

Having consulted the map, and seen that Liberec was some way from the nearest suitable airport, I looked at possible destinations, of which Dresden was one, but it soon became clear that Prague would be the place to go, and in fact the place to base myself. I again made arrangements to rendezvous with fellow fans in Prague, and set off early leaving on Wednesday 13th November, the day before the game.

Prague was cold but crisp, and I well remember arriving at the hotel and immediately setting off with my maps - Stanfords had done good trade with me over the past 15 months! – in search of culture. Prague is a beautiful city, and I understand it did not suffer greatly during WWII and so much of its architecture was unharmed by the ravages of 20th century war. On the Wednesday evening, I found and attended a classical music concert and - as in Moscow a year before - marvelled that I was in a foreign city listening to beautiful music, only 24 hours before the very different excitement of a football match! I strolled around the streets of Prague late into that evening, walking over the Charles Bridge and around the centre of the city and my over-riding memory is the sound of violins playing everywhere I went. Musicians were busking in shop doorways, playing hauntingly beautiful music, the like of which I had never heard elsewhere.

On the day of the game, and knowing that I had a few days in Prague with time to fill after the football match, I visited the National Theatre, housed in a stunning building on the banks of the Vlatava River and booked a ticket for a performance of Carmen that weekend. Notwithstanding the football match, this would prove to be the highlight of my trip.

For the game itself, fellow fans had booked a coach to take many of us to Liberec, and so we duly gathered at the meeting point and made our way to the northern reaches of the country. Having located the ground we made ourselves comfortable in a local bar and dreamed of our continued progress in the competition, made all the more realistic by being a goal ahead from the first leg.

However, the tactics employed on the night seemed to revolve around keeping a clean sheet, with no great attempt to score ourselves. Always a dangerous way to play, with such a slender lead, we nonetheless kept the game goalless until a couple of minutes from the end, when Slovan Liberec scored sending the tie into extra-time. Despite the introduction of Darren Bent, scorer in the first leg, and Finidi George, we were not able to change our

style of play on the night and it seemed inevitable that a penalty shoot-out would soon follow. And we all knew what happened when Ipswich were involved in penalties! Matt Holland got us off to a good start with the first spot-kick but from the moment Jermaine Wright's penalty was saved we were always playing catch up, and when Finidi George's kick was saved the game was all but up. It was a desperately sad way to end our run in Europe, and it was the manner in which we played that hurt most of all – one away goal would have left the hosts needing three, but our team was not set up to play for scoring and so we had a long and sombre journey back to the Czech capital.

Still, I had another couple of days to explore Prague and still had a night at the theatre to look forward to, which was a wonderfully grand occasion in another of Europe's many fine Opera Houses!

These six trips to the continent following Town over two seasons were each different in their own way, and collectively make a wonderful set of memories. To travel to Moscow and Milan, Scandinavia and Serbia, and the heart of Europe in the form of the Czech Republic and Luxembourg, and to do it following my team – our team – have given me experiences to last a lifetime.

Terry Hunt

Editor of the East Anglian Daily Times and a diehard Ipswich Town fan since 1968.

Like most Town fans, I was amazed when the Blues started their European journey in 1973. Could this really be my unglamorous, unsung, and frankly homespun team, competing with the most glamorous that Europe could offer? Well, yes it could – and we did rather well, didn't we?

My first foray abroad with the team came in the autumn of 1975, just a couple of weeks before I headed off to university, when my mate Roger Miller and I decided to go and watch Town take on mighty Feyenoord in Rotterdam.

Frankly, my memories of that trip are rather hazy (can't imagine why), but I do remember being on the coach waiting for the ferry at Felixstowe, and I also recall getting absolutely drenched during the game. It chucked it down, and the away fans – as always – were out in the open air.

We were standing (yes, it was that long ago) directly beneath some rather unpleasant home fans, who not only abused us from the first to the last minute, but also were adding to the precipitation with some rather warm liquid of their own. I'll leave it to your imagination…

Anyway, the game itself was a triumph, of course. Goals from David Johnson and Trevor Whymark saw us win 2-1 and set us on the way to a 4-1 aggregate victory, only for the team to come unstuck against Bruges in the next round.

As we boarded the coach for the long journey home, we were absolutely wet through. But we were 18, we'd had a beer and, most importantly, our team had won, so did we care about sleeping on the floor of the ferry? Did we heck!

By the time I made my next foray into Europe with Town, in late 1978, I'd got all sophisticated – or so I thought. My sister Karen and I boldly decided that we would fly to Innsbruck, where Town were defending a narrow 1-0 lead from the first leg at Portman Road.

We ended up on the same flight as the team, and I distinctly recall Trevor Whymark sporting a tight, curly perm, which were all the rage then. Who ever said that the 1970s was the decade that taste forgot?

This was the first experience of flying for both Karen and me, but, at the grand old age of 21, I decided that I must take responsibility for my 17-year-old sister. When our delicious in-flight meal arrived, I showed off my worldly-wise experience by pouring the tasty sauce all over my ham. It was only on the first taste that I realised the "sauce" was in fact custard. Credibility shot to pieces!

Innsbruck was, of course, snow-covered and beautiful. It had recently hosted the Winter Olympics and the giant ski jump was still in place. The mind boggles as to how anyone willingly throws themselves off something like that!

Town wobbled in the game itself. Innsbruck scored first, levelling the aggregate score, but George Burley popped up with a rare goal – nutmegging the keeper, as I recall, and Town held on despite the dismissal of Paul Mariner.

After that, some things called work, responsibility, and children came along in roughly that order to curtail any more trips with Town. But I have happy (if hazy) memories – and, who knows, maybe some future adventures to look forward to!

Graham Chenery

Having travelled to many away games in England, 'Chen' travelled with fellow season ticket holders to Helsingborg and Milan in 2001.

Helsingborgs

This was more enjoyable than Inter Milan, because the Swedish fans were very friendly and responded to the Ipswich fans very well, and there was no hint of trouble at all.

Club officials, including David Sheepshanks, mingled with the fans in the bars before the game.

There was a short ferry crossing to Denmark and we had no accommodation booked. We had planned to stay in Denmark but when we found out that the ferries ran all night we stayed in Helsingborg and mixed with the Ipswich and Swedish people. It was one of the best nights ever as away supporters, and although it wasn't planned that way it was accommodation problem solved!

Inter Milan

The trip to the San Siro was of course a highlight. We were aware of the reputation Italian fans had had when they met their British counterparts, remembering stories Town fans who went to Lazio and Roma had told, but times had changed and it was much more of a pleasure to go to any away game at home or abroad, so we weren't too worried.

But we had a mixed time of it. After the game some Inter fans came up to us in the street and smiling, told us how they admired the Town players, went into detail about the qualities of Titus Bramble and others, then wished us a pleasant flight home. As this was going on, one of them put his hand on my friend's arm in a friendly gesture and at the same time wrapped his right leg round his left leg. I thought, that's a bit strange, but thought nothing more of it. Later, we got to our hotel and went to buy some beers and as my friend, who was carrying all our money, went to his back pocket to pay, he found his wallet was missing. We searched high and low, retracing all our steps, but never found it. We assumed he must have been mugged by those so-called friendly fans.

Some other Golden Memories

Quite a lot of other people responded to our invitation to send us their memorable moments from their travels with Ipswich Town into Europe – and we are most grateful to them all. Here is a small selection of some that we have received …

Brian Polson of Braintree, has particular memories of town's first European trip – to Malta in 1962. He went on a two day trip with a flight from Southend on the Tuesday – well in advance of the match which was to kick off at 4.30pm next day, so they were given a tour of the Island in the morning. They stayed at the Imperial Hotel in Sliema but one of his travelling companions had a drink or two and had to be taken back to the hotel by some Maltese policemen. He fell fast asleep in his room and so managed to miss the whole match. Some officials from the rival Maltese club, Sliema Wanderers, however, heard of his plight and took him on a special island tour next day, ending at their own Stadium, and presenting him with some local memorabilia, so he didn't miss out too badly. Brian says his sister had married a British sailor and they were living in a flat over a bar which was frequented by football followers, so he and his mates were very well entertained and not allowed to buy a drink the whole time they were there. That, he says, was typical of the Maltese hospitality all the Ipswich supporters found.

John Booth, from Foxhall, is a keen photographer, and has hundreds of pictures of his numerous trips following Town. His special memory is of being at the top of a snowy mountain with Patrick Cobbold and David Rose among others.

Alan Reed, of Kirton also has photos, especially of Lansdkrona, in Sweden, where he also recalls taking part in the procession from the town centre to the Stadium following the local Pipe Band. Unfortunately, most of these pictures, after 30 years, are naturally a little faded, so we can only reproduce a few of them.

Tony Shaw, from Harwich, was a member of the Harwich Branch Supporters Committee and reckons the Leipzig trip was the best he did. He also recalls the excellent hospitality he and his friends were shown by the local people – especially students, keen to practice their English, who insisted on buying them drinks.

This is typical of the kind of relations our people developed all over Europe, and the reason why Ipswich supporters had the best reputation of any English club for their behaviour over the years.

Stuart Jarrold

Sports correspondent for BBC Radio / BBC TV and ITV Anglia and now with Sky Sports.

FC Bruges (UEFA Cup)

I was working for BBC national radio. Because Ipswich had let a 3-0 home win slip through their fingers, and lost the tie, I was asked, after the match, to do a piece over the phone for the 'Today' programme, to be broadcast the next morning.

By the time I was halfway through, the Stadium lights went out, and thus also the power. I found someone who could switch the power on again, but by this time I was running late. I was returning on the charter flight from Ostend to Southend with the Team and Press. I jumped in to a taxi and told him to drive hell for leather. He radioed his office, and asked them to phone the airport to get the flight delayed.

I arrived at the airport well after the departure time, and just ran through Customs and security, flashing my BBC ID card. Onto the tarmac, to see the plane being marshalled away from the stand, and taxi-ing away. I shouted , the marshalls waved their 'table tennis' bats and the plane stopped. The door opened - but it was 15 feet above the ground. The Marshals made a back for me to stand on, and Gerry Harrison (Anglia) and Neal Manning (Evening Star) hauled me onto the plane.

Lazio

The infamous 'Battle of the Olympic Stadium.' I wanted some 'after match comments' and made my way through to the dressing rooms. The Ipswich dressing room was locked, and it took a lot of persuading for someone to open the door enough for me to slip in. All hell was breaking out in the corridor outside. I got my quotes. There was a lot of drink in glass bottles in the dressing room, and Bobby Robson had told his players to keep one in their hands, and to defend themselves if the door was broken down.

More than an hour and a half later, we were escorted by riot police to the Team coach. I had to get a taxi to the BBC Rome office, and the team headed for the mountains for a quiet dinner.

UEFA Cup Final

Those iconic photos of the after match celebrations on the pitch, and in the dressing room, nearly didn't get taken.

My cameraman was also a brilliant professional photographer. We were due to film during the match, for Anglia News, and then he was to take after-match photo's for National newspapers.

The night before, together with a few other journalists, we were walking round the centre of Amsterdam, when we noticed my cameraman wasn't with us.

I was woken up at 3am by the police on the phone, saying he had been mugged. But his special prescription glasses had been smashed in the scuffle, and he couldn't see anything. Disaster!

Luckily we found a brilliant optician, who - in just 90 minutes - made some new glasses at the correct prescription, and the day was saved – just hours before the Final.

Gerry Harrison

Regular reporter and commentator on Town's European escapades and now a freelance journalist. Here he recalls some of the more eventful moments.

Twente Enschede (Oct 1974)

This game was due to be beamed back to Portman Road on a big screen, and the Football Club had sold thousands of tickets. I was contracted to commentate on the game for them, and had Phil Houseley as co-commentator. Phil was Chairman of the Supporters Club, but was also a Hospital Radio commentator at every Ipswich game.

When we arrived at the Stadium, nothing was set up. No cameras, no sound engineer - nothing. When I called back to Portman Road, the big screen was there and so was a big crowd. All they were seeing was an episode of Crossroads. We eventually discovered that the Irishman who had promoted the event had disappeared with all the gate receipts. The Club refunded everyone their ticket money.

Lokomotive Leipzig (March 1974)

I remember most the dire grey empty streets - the depressing buildings of this East German city. And yet, when we went inside the hotel, it was like stepping back to the 1930's. The hotel lounge was opulent, like a film set. And there sat half a dozen elderly ladies sipping tea, dressed in fur coats, jewellery, expensive clothes. Amazing. Of course the match was memorable, as was the visit the next day to Colditz Castle. I was covering the match for *The Times*, and was reminded recently of a line I wrote: 'The wheels of Lokomotive were beginning to turn!'

Oh dear!

FC Bruges (November 1975)

Stuart Jarrold has told you about how he almost missed the plane at Ostend airport. The Press and Players and Directors were travelling on the charter flight. Suddenly, as the aircraft was taxi-ing off the stand, one of the players noticed someone running out of the terminal and alongside the plane. It was Stuart, and as the plane stopped a stewardess opened the passenger door. It was a very long way down to the tarmac. As the tallest member of the Press party, I lay on the floor through the open door, while Neal Manning (Evening Star) held on to my ankles. We eventually dragged Stuart on to the plane, and all the players cheered!

In summary, although I covered both Ipswich

and Norwich for Anglia TV – we had a weekly Sunday extended highlights programme – I really loved the trips I made to the away European games with Ipswich. I made some good friends, had a lot of laughs, and shared the highs and lows with the fans and the players. Good times that we will never see again.

Peter Slater

These days BBC Radio Sports Reporter for the North of England, Peter remembers travelling with Ipswich Town during his time at Radio Orwell.

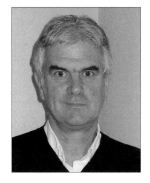

When I arrived in Suffolk in January 1981 Town were already in the quarter finals of the UEFA Cup. My first game, in St. Etienne, remains one of the most remarkable I've ever reported on. After the 4-1 win I was fortunate to be by the Dressing Room area as Eric Gates led the singing, I recorded it for a Friday night feature. Later on Allan Hunter took the microphone on the coach as the team made their way from Southend airport back to Portman Road. I sat there thinking, 'Is it always going to be this good?' Of course it wasn't, but we still had Cologne in the semis, where Bobby Robson took the team to a local Amusement Park to relax, and the final in Amsterdam.

After the win over Alkmaar, deep in the bowels of the Olympic Stadium, I was allowed into the dressing room, and sitting amongst the discarded kit and the towels, I interviewed Paul Mariner and Mick Mills.

When they paraded the Cup around the town I was on the bus, interviewing anyone and everyone. After just four and half months in Suffolk I'd experienced victory in Europe, an FA Cup semi final and that match in Middlesbrough where Bosco Jankovic deprived Town of the title.

Three months later we were back in Holland for a four team tournament. This time I travelled with the fans, first on the ferry to Zeebrugge, then by coach to Amsterdam.

One fan I particularly remember was a rotund gentleman called Barry, who took chain smoking to a new level. We'd watch him from the corner of the bar and time him to see just how long he could last between cigarettes. Sometimes it was less than a minute, but the nervous tics and the ritual of taking the fag out of the packet took up most of that.

The UEFA Cup wasn't kind to Town in the 81-82 season, as Alex Ferguson's Aberdeen knocked them out in the First Round. However we were able to enjoy a trip to a distillery near Huntly, along with the travelling fans.

By the following summer Bobby Robson had gone to manage England, although he did come

with the team on a pre-season tour to Florida, where I worked my passage by acting as a part-time courier on one of the fans' coaches. We spent much time on the white, sandy beaches in Clearwater, where I went running with Kevin Steggles. I also appeared on a local radio station phone-in, where one caller asked me "Do Norwich have a football team?".

In the UEFA Cup Town drew Roma. Robson came to Rome, where there was an awkward afternoon after he'd dropped Mick Mills from his first England squad. The team took in the sights, and Town's Dutch duo were often inseparable - wherever you went in Europe, you'd always see

Frans and Arnold out walking in the town. Roma was Ipswich's last competitive game in Europe for 19 years.

There were still pre-season tours, though. 1983 saw Dave Allard, of the Evening Star, and I taking in matches in Fredrikstad, Lillestrøm and Stavanger. The Radio Orwell car drove hundreds of miles through spectacular scenery. In Fredrikstad, I locked my keys in the car and had to be rescued by a Norwegian Policeman with what looked like a large table tennis bat. We later took Bobby Ferguson off for a swim in a fjord.

My final pre-season tour was in Holland, again on a Houseley organised coach trip. In Neuw-Lekkerland the ground was so small Dave Allard and I spent some time behind the goal talking to Mark Grew as Town won about 4-1. We stayed in Scheveningen, where I took the boys onto the nudist beach. They resolutely refused to take their clothes off.

I then moved on to the BBC, where I still cover lots of European football. Nowadays, unfortunately, we don't get the chance to mix with the fans like we used to, which is a shame.

Press matches

Philip recalls:

Neal Manning (*Evening Star*) and I used to organise friendly matches between the British Press and the Press from the country we were playing in Europe. Mel Henderson was the Captain and played in goal.

The most memorable of these games were played in Innsbruck, Oslo and Alkmaar. Innsbruck, because of the wonderful scenic ground we played on in the mountains. I remember both Bobby Robson and Bobby Ferguson playing in that game.

In Alkmaar, our guest player was Kieron Baker, the reserve keeper. The team and Press were staying in Amsterdam, at the Hilton (made infamous by John and Yoko Lennon). I happened to score the only goal of the game – and only because I was standing near the goal line, when a low cross hit me on the shin and went in! When we got back to the hotel, Bobby Robson was waiting in the Foyer, and asked Kieron the score.

'We won 1-0 Boss, Phil's shot almost hit the back of the net!'

In Oslo, the game was played at the University's stadium in front of an enthusiastic crowd of

RIGHT

The Press team for Innsbruck, 1978.
Back row from left – Brian Scovell (Daily Mail); Brian Woolnough (The Sun); Bobby Robson; Pete Barraclough (Radio Orwell); Mel Henderson (Ipswich Town PRO); Bobby Ferguson.
Front row – Phil Houseley (Felixstowe Travel); Tony Garnett (East Anglian Daily Times); Cyril Lea (First Team Coach); Neal Manning (Evening Star); Stuart Jarrold (Anglia TV).

students and first team players of the both UEFA Cup sides. In our team was Tony Gulliver (a long term fan and garage owner from Capel). He handled the ball in our area and Mel Henderson promptly sent him off, in spite of the fact we didn't have any substitutes! Minutes later Mel kicked air from a gentle back pass, and we were 2-0 down. At the beginning of the game, Mel told me to mark their left winger. Well, I hardly saw him all game. He was 6'6" tall, and had played the previous week for Lillestrøm against Rangers in the European Cup! I was wearing Reactolite glasses and it was a sunny afternoon. After the game, the Skeid Oslo Manager asked Bobby Robson who our right back was, adding 'He played quite well for a blind man'! I hung up my boots after that.